unconditional

unconditional

Gift (unconditional)

To

☐ Please read this. I want you to meet a friend of mine

☐ Please read this. I wish I had the courage to tell you more of this myself.

☐ Please read this. You need to make the most important decision of your life.

☐ Please read this. We know you don't agree with it all but please check it out.

☐ Please read this. I hope we can talk more afterwards.

☐ Please read this. We would like to invite you to...

Signed _____

(In the event of this being blank when you receive it feel free to fill it in, if and when you pass it on to a friend. You might have heard that you shouldn't keep good news to yourself)

unconditional

The GOSPEL OF MARK

from Today's New International Version

unconditional – the less important bit

by Nigel D. Pollock

Inter-Varsity Press
38 DeMontfort Street, Leicester LE2 1TD, England

British Library Cataloguing in Publication Data
A catalogue record for this book is available from the British Library.

ISBN 0-85111-292-7

Typeset by Avocet Typeset, Chilton, Aylesbury, Bucks
Printed in Great Britain by Cox & Wyman Ltd, Reading, Berkshire

Inter-Varsity Press is the publishing division of the Universities and Colleges Christian Fellowship (formerly the Inter-Varsity Fellowship), a student movement linking Christian Unions in universities and colleges throughout Great Britain, and a member movement of the International Fellowship of Evangelical Students. For more information about local and national activities write to UCCF, 38 De Montfort Street, Leicester LE1 7GP, email us at email@uccf.org.uk, or visit the UCCF website at www.uccf.org.uk.

Contents

I did not have a very successful time when I was at Oxford University. I missed my Blue and got a third. When I got my third I said to my Tutor: 'Did I get a third?' He replied: 'Yes, Rico.' 'Was I close to a 2:2?', I pleaded. 'No Rico, it was a very solid third.' So, I knew a job in the Church of England was my only career option!

Missing a rugby Blue, however, hurt me much more deeply. I first went to the Varsity Match as an eight-year-old schoolboy. That day I made it my ambition to one day play in that game at Twickenham. Twenty years later I was dropped ten days before the game. The other guy was a better player but it was still devastating – to not play in front of 65,000 people (the ground number in 1993). Being a Blue stays with you all your life. In rugby circles it is a marker which is universally respected. Having grown up in these circles I desperately wanted that distinction. I wanted it for myself, my parents, my friends, my schoolteachers and felt my whole identity had been battered when I was not selected.

And it is moments like that which take you to your core values, which make you reach into your own soul and ask: Why do I really matter? Why am I really significant? Where is my strength? *Unconditional* says so much about the journey I had to make when I was at Oxford. I wholeheartedly commend it to you – I am now so glad I missed my Blue so that I might know my true value.

Rico Tice

What kind of book is this?

It is a shocking, dangerous and extraordinary book.

It is a book you should read. It deals with events of cosmic and eternal significance that affect you, your friends and your family.

Who wrote this book?

The important parts of this book were written a long time ago by a young man called Mark. The other parts of this were written fairly recently by a man called Nigel who isn't young exactly but can't quite accept the description 'middle aged'. Mark was from the Middle East. Nigel is from Scotland. As you would expect from this brief amount of biographical information Mark is far more articulate. He was also inspired in a unique way by the Holy Spirit as he wrote. Nigel was not inspired in the same way but was helped by his friends and harassed by his editor until he finished his part. You can contact Nigel at Nigel@uccf.org.uk. Mark unfortunately is not on email.

Why 'Unconditional'?

God loves extravagantly. Like no one you have ever known. Mind blowing generosity, incredible patience, breathtaking imagination and unbelievable cost. God loves unconditionally. God's love is not conditional on your appearance, your performance or your popularity. It is not extended only to those of a specific gender, race or family background. God's love cannot be earned or bought. God loves you, whoever you are, whatever you have done and wherever you are from. You may not feel like God could or should love you but he does. You may not think that God's love has any relevance to you, but it has. The love of God is not sentimental – it translates into powerful action. The Bible explains that the God who created us did not abandon us, even though we abandoned him, but instead chose to mount the most remarkable and audacious rescue mission in the history of humanity. He loved the world so much that he sent his only son to die in our place.

Unconditional love
Amazing love. God's love. For you!

This book will not answer all your questions. There are a couple of reasons for this. One is that the whole of who God is and what he has done cannot be contained in one short volume. The other is that there are loads of things that I just do not know. My intention is very specific – it is simply to provide you with an introduction to Jesus.

In these pages you will meet some ordinary people who have received that unconditional love and long that you would do the same.

Their desire, like mine, is that you would meet the person that God sent – his own son.

Our sincere hope and prayer is that you would not just know more about Jesus but that you would come to know him personally.

The unconditional love of God is not about an old religion – it is about a new relationship. You will have to decide if this is for you. But be in no doubt that this is the single most important issue that you will face in your whole life.

Response

I had been asked to speak at an open meeting in the Student Union. Christian Union members had invited their friends to come and there was a good crowd gathered. I spoke from Mark's Gospel about the cross and new life in Christ. At the end of the evening a student approached me. The conversation went something like this:

'You were saying that it is really important that we think about Jesus for ourselves?'

'Yes I was.'

'Well, if it is such an important message, why didn't they ask a decent speaker to explain it?'

'It is certainly a great message and I don't think any of us would claim to be able to explain it adequately.'

'So you admit you are inadequate – that's even worse. And another thing, why were you reading out of that little book? We get enough books during the week.'

'It is important to me to show that what I am saying comes from somewhere. I didn't make the message up, I just pass it on.'

'Well if they ask you again, do us all a favour and just say no, OK!'

People respond to the message in many different ways. Speaking with people in situations just like that, I have seen a lot of different responses. Many could not articulate what had made them respond in the way they did. Some start following Jesus when they never thought they would. Others find it gets under their skin like an itch and they start thinking about it over and over. Others still argue and get angry but are not sure why. The response may be faith or it may be anger but _the truth is that you have to make a response to Jesus_. You simply cannot be ambivalent about this man.

I can't promise to tell you things that you will like to read. It may not be an easy message. Encountering Jesus is seldom a comfortable thing. You may wish by the end that I hadn't bothered trying. But please stick with it. I didn't make this stuff up – in my inadequate way I am trying to point you to Jesus and I believe that he has something to say to you.

Will the real Jesus please stand up?
Many people have an opinion about the identity of Jesus. Some say he was a great teacher or philosopher, some a revolutionary, some say he is the Son of God, others a prophet, others still a myth or legend.

It seems to me that there are too many people in the world telling you what to believe and how to live and what to think and what to do.

Too many people are willing to accept second hand ideas and presuppositions. I think it is vital that you have the courage and the audacity to consider first hand the historical facts and to come to an informed decision.

The stakes are extremely high. What is on the line is nothing less than your eternal destiny. Surely that is something that is worth investing a little bit of time investigating for yourself!

The obvious place to start is with the original source documents. The people who were there experienced life with Jesus at close quarters. Their testimony places Jesus in a historical and cultural context. They may not be able to explain everything but they can at least tell us what they saw.

In this book is the whole text of one of the eyewitness accounts of the life of Jesus. Someone who lived through these times, and whose sources were those closest to the action, wrote it. It was the first account of the life and death of Jesus to be written and circulated. Its author was Mark. There are three other accounts of the life of Christ recorded by Matthew, Luke and John. These complementary accounts are well worth reading as they throw greater light on the life and work of Christ. If you have a Bible you will find them clustered together at the start of the New Testament. These ancient texts communicate a powerful, contemporary, life-changing truth.

REAL LIVES

Paul Gibson reads History at St Catherine's College, Oxford.

For the first twenty years of my life I was definitely not a Christian. God seemed like a concept that desperate people had invented to calm their fears of dying. Christians were people holding extraordinary and deluded views and I was glad that I could rise above such nonsense.

Such was my confidence in my atheism that, when a friend asked me along to a talk about Jesus, I accepted, sure that I could quickly pick holes in their attempts to justify

Christianity. It didn't change my mind, but it was interesting enough that my friend persuaded me to return for further talks. By the end, I still thought Christianity was probably false, but decided to think about it more. I needed to be absolutely certain whether it was true or false. If it really was true, then my rejection of God would have eternally disas-trous consequences.

My friend found an enquirers' course for me to do, organ-ized by one of the local churches. I turned up each week, armed with my supposedly infallible atheist punch-lines. To my surprise, none of the questions foxed the Christians there. They had actually thought these issues through, and still believed the claims of Christ. I gradually realized that Jesus must have been who he claimed to be: the Son of God. I saw that, against all my expectations, Christianity really was true, and I was guilty before God. Finally I accepted Jesus into my life, as my Lord and Saviour.

Since I became a Christian my life has felt so fulfilled. Little things that used to matter a lot don't upset me any more, because I have a relationship with Jesus that rides above everything else. It's not always easy – I still keep on doing things that Jesus doesn't like, and feel really guilty when I do. But knowing that God has forgiven me through Jesus' amazing sacrifice is incredible. I wouldn't go back now for the world.

Mark's biography of Jesus falls into four main sections. The full text of each section is printed in full here, so that his whole book is included. If you only read some bits of this book read those. I have made some comments on selected passages. These parts are not more important but they may contain elements that benefit from some background explanation or are of particular significance in the narrative.

Introducing the main characters

John Mark. A young man with a literary bent. John is a Jewish name and Mark a Greek one. His mates called him Mark, his mum probably called him John. He may have witnessed some of the events in Jerusalem first hand. Part of Paul and Barnabus' mission team until he was the cause of a major falling out. Wrote the Gospel which he fortunately called Mark. It would have left John in a very awkward position if the name John's Gospel had already been taken.

John the Baptist. Prophet with absolutely no interest in fashion or gastronomy. His mother Elizabeth was cousin to Jesus' mother Mary and the two women, although very different in age, were pregnant at around the same time. His habit of wearing camel hair shirts and eating locusts and honey would have been excellent preparation for *Survivor*. John's message of repentance did not endear him to the authorities and he was eliminated early not long after Jesus' baptism. Imprisoned for a time before King Herod had him beheaded as a party favour.

Isaiah. Major prophet during the expansion of the Assyrian Empire from about 740 to 680 BC although that wasn't what they thought the date was at the time. Israel is invaded and Jerusalem threatened and Isaiah writes about its future capture, the exile of its people and their future return. His key themes are judgement and salvation. He looks forward to a king descended from David ruling in righteousness, a suffering servant, and a new Jerusalem as a focus for all nations. The New Testament writers understood Jesus to be the fulfilment of many of these prophecies.

Daniel. Early international student. Daniel was one of the first wave of bright and promising Jews taken into captivity in Babylon after the fall of Jerusalem. He is promoted to a senior position in the Babylonian civil service, a job made more interesting by his desire to honour God. The first half of his book details his adventures in Babylon – the second is a special type of literature concerning the end of time. He emphasized the sovereignty of God over kings and empires and wrote about God's chosen one establishing a kingdom where he would reign forever. In a bit of an 'X-File' the time prophesied from the decree to rebuild the temple to the coming of God's anointed, 483 years, works out to the time of Jesus' ministry.

Malachi. Italian sounding prophet writing around 433 BC. The Assyrian Empire has been defeated by the Babylonian Empire which in turn has been defeated by the Persian Empire. (Ancient history wasn't just Egyptians, Greeks and Romans you know!) The exiles return and the temple rebuilding commences but the people are still unfaithful to God. Malachi calls them to repentance and looks forward to the coming of the Lord who will purify the priests and judge the people. His writing becomes the last book in the Old Testament. Jesus does not arrive until 400 years later.

Nero. Roman Emperor who gave violinists a bad name by playing as his capital burned. The fire destroyed large sections of Rome in AD 64. Nero like many Roman Emperors wasn't quite the full Euro and word on the street was that he may have started the fire himself. Looking for a convenient scapegoat he blamed the Christians. It was the start of a great persecution, during which many Christians lost their lives, probably including Peter and Paul.

Peter. Fisherman called Simon to whom Jesus gave a new name and a new vocation. He was to be 'The Rock' which rather than being a WWF professional wrestler meant he was going to be part of the foundation of the church. Peter behaves in a most un-rock-like manner after Jesus' arrest when, as predicted, he denies Jesus three times. But Jesus does not write Peter off and restores him after the resurrection. Peter became an important figure in the early church and two of his letters, the first written at the time of the persecution in Rome, are in the New Testament. He was the key source for Mark's Gospel account.

Disciples. A group Jesus called to follow him. It was a common concept for spiritual teachers to have a group of disciples – John the Baptist had a few for example. Mark often refers to Jesus disciples as 'the twelve', which was a good name because there were twelve of them. Jesus' small group included: two sets of fishing brothers, Peter and Andrew, and James and John, as well as a tax collector, a freedom fighter and the purse keeper, Judas, who was turned to become an enemy mole and would later betray Jesus. For some of the disciples we get biographical information and some dialogue or action is recorded – for others all we know are their names. Most of them died premature and violent deaths as they spread the news of Jesus' resurrection.

Pharisees. Influential Jewish sect. Their position was to hold that everything in the oral tradition was as inspired and authoritative as the *Torah* or written law. This put human tradition on the same level as divine revelation. For example when they complain that Jesus is breaking the Sabbath what they mean is that he is breaking their interpretation of what was and was not allowed on the Sabbath. This kind of stuff ran for pages and pages as it sought to cover every conceivable eventuality. The Pharisees' distinctives were strong ethical teaching, belief in life after death and angels, and on not being the Sadducees.

Elijah. Prophet of Israel during the reign of Ahab 874–853 BC a time of great spiritual conflict. His defeat of the prophets of Baal earns him a kind of 'Braveheart' status in the history of Israel. He does not die but is taken to be with God in a fiery chariot (swinging low!). His return was prophesied by Malachi. This accounts for the public speculation that Jesus might be Elijah. Jesus ties John the Baptist into this prophecy. Interestingly Elijah himself appears on the Mount of Transfiguration with Moses and Jesus. A point which Mark makes very little out of.

Herod. Family of puppet kings. Herod the Great, most likely his own choice of name, was first appointed by the Roman

Senate in 40 BC. He murdered the babies in Bethlehem who were born at the same time as Jesus. Thereafter it starts getting complicated. The family ruled for four generations – each generation had a King Herod. For a time three of the sons of Herod the Great ruled in different parts of the region, two of them were called King Herod. These are a lot of Herods to keep track of. The Herod who had John the Baptist killed was Herod Philip I and the Herod to whom Pilate sent Jesus was Herod Antipas. Already your eyes may be glazing over, suffice it to say they were not a very pleasant dynasty and seem about as bad as each other.

Pilate. Roman Provincial Governor of Judea from AD 26 to AD 36. According to legend born in Scotland, something he keeps pretty quiet about in the gospels. (In fact given what he does say in the gospels it is maybe something I should keep quiet about!) While Herod and the Jewish Council had some influence he was the supreme power and he was the law. Ultimately Pilate has the power of life and death in his area of government. Unable to find any reason for the charge against Jesus he tried to set him free but was swayed by the mob and sentenced Jesus to be flogged and put to death.

Mark is the first gospel to hit the streets. Written some-where about 64AD at a time when many of the eyewitnesses to the Jesus events were still alive.

It was the shortest of the four gospel accounts and moves rapidly from one event to the next. The Greek word, which is variously translated as 'immediately' or 'at once' or 'just then', is used nearly fifty times in the narrative. It is a vibrant, roller coaster of episodes rushing through the life of Jesus.

It was written at a time of great persecution for the early church under the Roman Emperor Nero. The oral tradition was being eroded as increasing numbers of believers who knew Jesus personally faced death for their faith. The church leaders in Rome recognized that a written account must be made while there was still time. John Mark who grew up in Jerusalem in a Jewish family was given the task. One of the key sources to whom he had access was Peter, one of Jesus' inner circle. Jesus gathered a group of friends about him at the start of his travel-ling ministry. The core of this little community was the twelve disciples and within that Peter, James and John were taken by Jesus into a number of situations where the others did not go. Peter has seen as much of Jesus as anybody on earth.

Mark starts with the headlines, immediately putting down a marker for the subject and scope of this story.

The headlines in a newspaper seek to capture the essence of what the lead story is that day. In the event it is often possible to tell something about the magnitude of the story from the headline. So when the pre World Cup headline read, 'Beckham breaks foot!' we were in no doubt who or what was the focus of the story. It was not some un-named local footballer it was the captain of England. It was not a minor injury it was a broken bone. It was not his hand or his hair which were injured – it was the golden foot in the embroidered boot which conjures spectacular free kicks. We were dealing with an event potentially affecting the manifest destiny of England.

Headline writers are concerned to sell newspapers and the headlines often focus on the relevance of the story. Many provincial newspapers had the headlines, 'Local Man Lost at Sea' when the Titanic went down. Such stories are told against the parochial attitude of the local press, but while not helping you grasp the scale of the story, they do pinpoint its relevance.

Mark goes into print with the biggest news story of all time and it is directly relevant to you. Right from the start he goes straight to the heart of the matter. This is the beginning – not just the beginning of what Mark is writing but the beginning of the gospel or 'good news'. The good news Mark describes is focused on a person. This is not an abstract philosophical treatise or a disembodied idea. The good news is about Jesus Christ. Mark immediately comments on Jesus' identity – his central concern. Mark is not trying to write a conventional biography in the sense of childhood, rise to fame, achievements and perspective. This is not something of local interest – his headline is not 'Jesus Christ – the Greatest Galilean who ever lived'. It is a headline that states something which, if it is true, is absolutely incredible in its substance and universal in its application.

Mark's headline is 'Jesus Christ, the Son of God'. This is potentially confusing language. In Jesus' day it was sometimes used as a religious way of saying 'human being' but here it is clear that the meaning is specific. Mark chooses his words with care. He is not just using this terminology to indicate that Jesus is a man or even 'The Man'. He has concluded that there is more to Jesus' identity than his humanity.

Jesus Christ is the Son of God

It is difficult for us to appreciate the enormity of this statement. The cornerstone of Jewish identity is the statement, 'Hear, O Israel: The LORD our God, the LORD is one' (Deuteronomy 6.4). To announce that someone is his son is to challenge that which the culture holds most sacred. It is beyond announcing in a Glasgow pub that you think England are a decent team and you wish them well. It is worse than burning the American flag on Capitol Hill on the 4th of July when the President is there. It is on a level with denouncing the Koran at a Taliban mosque during Ramadan.

This is a shocking headline which would have caused some of its first readers to gasp. We must not allow familiarity with the language to dull our senses – it is still a remarkable statement. It is rendered all the more shocking to those first readers by the manner of Jesus' death. It was common knowledge that Jesus had been crucified. This was an abomination to civilized thinking. To be crucified was to be disgraced and considered disgusting. Yet Mark boldly declares that this pariah is nothing less than the Son of God.

What could have led Mark to such a revolutionary conclusion? It is time to start reading his words.

MARK 1.1–13

John the Baptist prepares the way

1 The beginning of the good news about Jesus the Messiah, ²as it is written in Isaiah the prophet:

"I *will send my messenger ahead of you,*

  who will prepare your way" –

³"*a voice of one calling in the desert,*

'*Prepare the way for the Lord,*

  make straight paths for him.'" (Isaiah 40.3)

⁴And so John the Baptist appeared in the desert region, preaching a baptism of repentance for the forgiveness of sins. ⁵The whole Judean countryside and all the people of Jerusalem went out to him. Confessing their sins, they were baptised by him in the River Jordan. ⁶John wore clothing made of camel's hair, with a leather belt round his waist, and he ate locusts and wild honey. ⁷And this was his message: "After me comes the one more powerful than I, the thongs of whose sandals I am not worthy to stoop down and untie. ⁸I baptise you with water, but he will baptise you with the Holy Spirit."

The baptism and testing of Jesus

⁹At that time Jesus came from Nazareth in Galilee and

was baptised by John in the Jordan. [10]Just as Jesus was coming up out of the water, he saw heaven being torn open and the Spirit descending on him like a dove. [11]And a voice came from heaven: "You are my Son, whom I love; with you I am well pleased."

[12]At once the Spirit sent him out into the desert, [13]and he was in the desert for forty days, being tempted by Satan. He was with the wild animals, and angels attended him.

[continued on page 32]

Truth is stranger than fiction

Stop and think for a moment about Mark's staggering statement. His headline claim is that this man who walked the shores of Galilee 2000 years ago has a divine identity. I do not know if you believe in the existence of God or if you have any ideas as to what God may be like. Here is a claim that demands some consideration. A writer from a Jewish, monotheistic background claims that the man Jesus is the Son of God. According to his worldview this could be nothing short of blasphemy. It is like someone today claiming to be a prophet greater than Mohammed or to be the Jewish Messiah. It would not go down very well! Far from backing away from this Mark straight away backs it up to leave us in no doubt what he is saying.

That's prophetic

The Jewish prophets looked forward to a day when God would send the promised one to deliver his people. Mark places the life of Jesus into the context of Old Testament prophecy. He mentions the ancient prophet Isaiah by name but actually combines a verse from Malachi, another Old Testament writer, in his quotation from Isaiah. The quote speaks of a day when a messenger will appear, in the desert, preparing the way for the Lord. Mark understands that John the Baptist was the promised messenger and that Jesus is the Lord spoken about in these prophecies. The identity of Jesus is intrinsically connected to the Old Testament revelation of God's promises and plans. Jesus coming was not a bolt from the blue – it is firmly located in the promises that the God of Abraham, Isaac and Jacob made with His chosen people Israel.

Locust and honey surprise

The voice crying in the desert had a specific message to proclaim. John called people to 'repentance'. Repentance may be an unfamiliar term; it is a word that is about a change of direction and thinking. John was saying to the people, 'Stop living life under your own steam and turn to God – show God you are serious about the wrong things in your life.' Crowds gathered to hear him, many responded and were baptized in the River Jordan. John in human terms was a success but it was not his intention to found 'John the Baptist Ministries' and to be the focus of attention. He is clear in his preaching to the crowd that someone else is coming. His job was to point people to Jesus. The one who was coming was going to do things on a different level. John was baptizing with water but the expected one would baptize with the Holy Spirit. Whatever Jesus is going to do is going to be spiritual and is going to be inextricably linked with the Holy Spirit.

People in London, Edinburgh and other cities stand at

pavement junctions holding up big 'Golf Sale' signs with an arrow pointing in the direction of the often temporary shop. It does not strike me as the most exciting job in the world but it does tell you where the golf sale is happening. The man with the sign cannot provide you with anything but he can point you to the place where you can find what you are looking for. John the Baptist held up the sign pointing the way to Jesus. He was not the truth, he knew the truth and he testified to the one who was coming after him, who was the truth.

A Christian friend may have given you this book, perhaps not with wild clothes and munching locusts! (although there are no guarantees – the Christian faith is not a cause of weirdness but it is not an antidote to it either.) Christians seek to walk in this heritage of being a signpost pointing you to Jesus with the desire that you might find truth, life and access to God.

Unusual day at the office

One day Jesus came to the Jordan river. He associated himself with the message and ministry of John and identified himself with those being baptized. To John's surprise Jesus asked to be baptized and, as he came out of the water, something amazing happened. God the Holy Spirit descended on him like a dove and a voice spoke from heaven, 'This is my son, whom I love; with him I am well pleased' (Matthew 3.17). This is astonishing. The unique nature of Jesus is affirmed by God himself. Publicly God confirms Jesus' relationship with him, his love for him and his pleasure with him. Jesus has lived a sinless life to this point; this is why John sensed it was inappropriate somehow for

Jesus to be baptized. This incident gives an insight into the nature of God. In a way which is beyond the capacity of any analogy to explain God is one but is also three. All three members of the Trinity are explicitly mentioned at this event. God the father, whose voice is heard, Jesus the son who is baptised and the Holy Spirit who descends. This is not the kind of thing that happens every day! Already there is a sense that we are listening to something very important. Jesus immediately heads into the desert where he endures temptation as he prepares for what is to come next.

Mark has made some big claims in his headlines. Claims need to be substantiated. Many people through history have made claims about themselves. There needs to be a process of verification to establish if these are credible. Prophecy can be applied easily enough to current events or personalities – look at the way the writings of Nostradamus have been interpreted and applied. Events can be staged to fool or impress the ordinary person. In a desert, inspired by a charismatic preacher, mass hallucination or self-delusion may occur. Mark's headlines certainly grab your attention but we need to check out if the story is as big as he says.

The headline's function, whether real or apocryphal, is to make you want to read on. Are you up for a bit more?

Getting the big picture

For our tenth wedding anniversary Ailsa and I spent a long weekend in Paris with some friends. One of our favourite places was the Musée d'Orsay where many stunning impressionist paintings are on display. When you stand right up close to the picture you can see the individual dots of colour. A close examination of one section could almost lead you to the conclusion that what you are looking at is a selection of random dots. It is only when you stand back that you realize that there is a pattern and that the artist has chosen to place each dot in relationship to the others with the intention of producing an image. The picture becomes clear as you see how the individual dots contribute to the whole work.

Mark selects incidents from the life of Jesus. He tells us about specific things that Jesus said and did. Many events are recorded but the intention is that the reader will be able to see how these details combine to create a picture of the identity of Jesus. The miracles, the teaching, the claims all contribute to our understanding and serve to clarify who Jesus is.

As you read this section the key question to be asking yourself is 'Who is this?' It was a question that the disciples asked, 'Who is this? Even the wind and waves obey him?' (Mark 4.41). It is a question Jesus himself explores, 'Who do people say I am?' (Mark 8.27). It is a question that he addresses directly to his disciples, 'What about you? Who do you say that I am?' It is *the* question on which you have to come to a decision.

[continued from page 27]
MARK 1.14–8.30

Jesus announces the good news

¹⁴After John was put in prison, Jesus went into Galilee, proclaiming the good news of God. ¹⁵"The time has come," he said. "The kingdom of God has come near. Repent and believe the good news!"

Jesus calls his first disciples

¹⁶As Jesus walked beside the Sea of Galilee, he saw Simon and his brother Andrew casting a net into the lake, for they were fishermen. ¹⁷"Come, follow me," Jesus said, "and I will send you out to catch people." ¹⁸At once they left their nets and followed him.

¹⁹When he had gone a little farther, he saw James son of Zebedee and his brother John in a boat, preparing their nets. ²⁰Without delay he called them, and they left their father Zebedee in the boat with the hired men and followed him.

Jesus drives out an evil spirit

²¹They went to Capernaum, and when the Sabbath

came, Jesus went into the synagogue and began to teach. [22]The people were amazed at his teaching, because he taught them as one who had authority, not as the teachers of the law. [23]Just then a man in their synagogue who was possessed by an evil spirit cried out, [24]"What do you want with us, Jesus of Nazareth? Have you come to destroy us? I know who you are—the Holy One of God!"

[25]"Be quiet!" said Jesus sternly. "Come out of him!" [26]The evil spirit shook the man violently and came out of him with a shriek.

[27]The people were all so amazed that they asked each other, "What is this? A new teaching—and with authority! He even gives orders to evil spirits and they obey him." [28]News about him spread quickly over the whole region of Galilee.

Jesus heals many

[29]As soon as they left the synagogue, they went with James and John to the home of Simon and Andrew. [30]Simon's mother-in-law was in bed with a fever, and they immediately told Jesus about her. [31]So he went to her, took her hand and helped her up. The fever left her and she began to wait on them.

[32]That evening after sunset the people brought to Jesus all who were ill and demon-possessed. [33]The whole town gathered at the door, [34]and Jesus healed many who had various diseases. He also drove out many demons, but he would not let the demons speak because they knew who he was.

Jesus prays in a solitary place

35Very early in the morning, while it was still dark, Jesus got up, left the house and went off to a solitary place, where he prayed. 36Simon and his companions went to look for him, 37and when they found him, they exclaimed: "Everyone is looking for you!"

38Jesus replied, "Let us go somewhere else—to the nearby villages—so that I can preach there also. That is why I have come." 39So he travelled throughout Galilee, preaching in their synagogues and driving out demons.

Jesus heals a man with leprosy

40A man with leprosy came to him and begged him on his knees, "If you are willing, you can make me clean."

41Jesus was indignant. He reached out his hand and touched the man. "I am willing," he said. "Be clean!" 42Immediately the leprosy left him and he was cleansed.

43Jesus sent him away at once with a strong warning: 44"See that you don't tell this to anyone. But go, show your-self to the priest and offer the sacrifices that Moses commanded for your cleansing, as a testimony to them." 45Instead he went out and began to talk freely, spreading the news. As a result, Jesus could no longer enter a town openly but stayed outside in lonely places. Yet the people still came to him from everywhere.

Jesus forgives and heals a paralysed man

2 A few days later, when Jesus again entered Capernaum, the people heard that he had come home. 2So many gathered that there was no room left, not even outside the

door, and he preached the word to them. ³Some men came, bringing to him a paralysed man, carried by four of them. ⁴Since they could not get him to Jesus because of the crowd, they made an opening in the roof above Jesus by digging through it and then lowered the mat the man was lying on. ⁵When Jesus saw their faith, he said to the paralysed man, "Son, your sins are forgiven."

⁶Now some teachers of the law were sitting there, thinking to themselves, ⁷"Why does this fellow talk like that? He's blaspheming! Who can forgive sins but God alone?"

⁸Immediately Jesus knew in his spirit that this was what they were thinking in their hearts, and he said to them, "Why are you thinking these things? ⁹Which is easier: to say to this paralysed man, 'Your sins are forgiven,' or to say, 'Get up, take your mat and walk'? ¹⁰But I want you to know that the Son of Man has authority on earth to forgive sins." So he said to the man, ¹¹"I tell you, get up, take your mat and go home." ¹²He got up, took his mat and walked out in full view of them all. This amazed everyone and they praised God, saying, "We have never seen anything like this!"

Jesus calls Levi and eats with sinners

¹³Once again Jesus went out beside the lake. A large crowd came to him, and he began to teach them. ¹⁴As he walked along, he saw Levi son of Alphaeus sitting at the tax collector's booth. "Follow me," Jesus told him, and Levi got up and followed him.

¹⁵While Jesus was having dinner at Levi's house, many tax collectors and "sinners" were eating with him and his disciples, for there were many who followed him. ¹⁶When

the teachers of the law who were Pharisees saw him eating with the "sinners" and tax collectors, they asked his disciples: "Why does he eat with tax collectors and 'sinners'?"

17On hearing this, Jesus said to them, "It is not the healthy who need a doctor, but those who are ill. I have not come to call the righteous, but sinners."

Jesus questioned about fasting

18Now John's disciples and the Pharisees were fasting. Some people came and asked Jesus, "How is it that John's disciples and the disciples of the Pharisees are fasting, but yours are not?"

19Jesus answered, "How can the guests of the bridegroom fast while he is with them? They cannot, so long as they have him with them. 20But the time will come when the bridegroom will be taken from them, and on that day they will fast.

21"No-one sews a patch of unshrunk cloth on an old garment. If they do, the new piece will pull away from the old, making the tear worse. 22And people do not pour new wine into old wineskins. If they do, the wine will burst the skins, and both the wine and the wineskins will be ruined. No, they pour new wine into new wineskins."

Jesus is Lord of the Sabbath

23One Sabbath Jesus was going through the cornfields, and as his disciples walked along, they began to pick some ears of corn. 24The Pharisees said to him, "Look, why are they doing what is unlawful on the Sabbath?"

²⁵He answered, "Have you never read what David did when he and his companions were hungry and in need? ²⁶In the days of Abiathar the high priest, he entered the house of God and ate the consecrated bread, which is lawful only for priests to eat. And he also gave some to his companions."

²⁷Then he said to them, "The Sabbath was made for people, not people for the Sabbath. ²⁸So the Son of Man is Lord even of the Sabbath."

Jesus heals on the Sabbath

3 Another time he went into the synagogue, and a man with a shrivelled hand was there. ²Some of them were looking for a reason to accuse Jesus, so they watched him closely to see if he would heal him on the Sabbath. ³Jesus said to the man with the shrivelled hand, "Stand up in front of everyone."

⁴Then Jesus asked them, "Which is lawful on the Sabbath: to do good or to do evil, to save life or to kill?" But they remained silent.

⁵He looked around at them in anger and, deeply distressed at their stubborn hearts, said to the man, "Stretch out your hand." He stretched it out, and his hand was completely restored. ⁶Then the Pharisees went out and began to plot with the Herodians how they might kill Jesus.

Crowds follow Jesus

⁷Jesus withdrew with his disciples to the lake, and a large crowd from Galilee followed. ⁸When they heard all he was doing, many people came to him from Judea, Jerusalem, Idumea, and the regions across the Jordan and

around Tyre and Sidon. ⁹Because of the crowd he told his disciples to have a small boat ready for him, to keep the people from crowding him. ¹⁰For he had healed many, so that those with diseases were pushing forward to touch him. ¹¹Whenever the evil spirits saw him, they fell down before him and cried out, "You are the Son of God."

¹²But he gave them strict orders not to tell others about him.

Jesus appoints the twelve

¹³Jesus went up on a mountainside and called to him those he wanted, and they came to him. ¹⁴He appointed twelve that they might be with him and that he might send them out to preach ¹⁵and to have authority to drive out demons. ¹⁶These are the twelve he appointed: Simon (to whom he gave the name Peter); ¹⁷James son of Zebedee and his brother John (to them he gave the name Boanerges, which means Sons of Thunder); ¹⁸Andrew, Philip, Bartholomew, Matthew, Thomas, James son of Alphaeus, Thaddaeus, Simon the Zealot ¹⁹and Judas Iscariot, who betrayed him.

Jesus accused by his family and by teachers of the law

²⁰Then Jesus entered a house, and again a crowd gathered, so that he and his disciples were not even able to eat. ²¹When his family heard about this, they went to take charge of him, for they said, "He is out of his mind."

²²And the teachers of the law who came down from Jerusalem said, "He is possessed by Beelzebul! By the prince of demons he is driving out demons."

[23]So Jesus called them over to him and began to speak to them in parables: "How can Satan drive out Satan? [24]If a kingdom is divided against itself, that kingdom cannot stand. [25]If a house is divided against itself, that house cannot stand. [26]And if Satan opposes himself and is divided, he cannot stand; his end has come. [27]In fact, no-one can enter a strong man's house without first tying him up. Then he can plunder the strong man's house. [28]Truly I tell you, people will be forgiven all their sins and all the blasphemies they utter. [29]But whoever blasphemes against the Holy Spirit will never be forgiven, but is guilty of an eternal sin."

[30]He said this because they were saying, "He has an evil spirit."

[31]Then Jesus' mother and brothers arrived. Standing outside, they sent someone in to call him. [32]A crowd was sitting round him, and they told him, "Your mother and brothers are outside looking for you."

[33]"Who are my mother and my brothers?" he asked.

[34]Then he looked at those seated in a circle round him and said, "Here are my mother and my brothers! [35]Whoever does God's will is my brother and sister and mother."

The parable of the sower

4 Again Jesus began to teach by the lake. The crowd that gathered round him was so large that he got into a boat and sat in it out on the lake, while all the people were along the shore at the water's edge. [2]He taught them many things by parables, and in his teaching said: [3]"Listen! A farmer went out to sow his seed. [4]As he was scattering the seed, some fell along the path, and the birds came and ate it up.

⁵Some fell on rocky places, where it did not have much soil. It sprang up quickly, because the soil was shallow. ⁶But when the sun came up, the plants were scorched, and they withered because they had no root. ⁷Other seed fell among thorns, which grew up and choked the plants, so that they did not bear grain. ⁸Still other seed fell on good soil. It came up, grew and produced a crop, some multiplying thirty, some sixty, some a hundred times."

⁹Then Jesus said, "Whoever has ears to hear, let them hear."

¹⁰When he was alone, the Twelve and the others around him asked him about the parables. ¹¹He told them, "The secret of the kingdom of God has been given to you. But to those on the outside everything is said in parables ¹²so that,

> " 'they may be ever seeing but never perceiving,
> and ever hearing but never understanding;
> otherwise they might turn and be forgiven!'"
> (Isaiah 6.9,10)

¹³Then Jesus said to them, "Don't you understand this parable? How then will you understand any parable? ¹⁴The farmer sows the word. ¹⁵Some people are like seed along the path, where the word is sown. As soon as they hear it, Satan comes and takes away the word that was sown in them. ¹⁶Others, like seed sown on rocky places, hear the word and at once receive it with joy. ¹⁷But since they have no root, they last only a short time. When trouble or persecution comes because of the word, they quickly fall away. ¹⁸Still others, like seed sown among thorns, hear the word; ¹⁹but the worries of this life, the deceitfulness of wealth and the desires for other things come in and choke the

word, making it unfruitful. [20]Others, like seed sown on good soil, hear the word, accept it, and produce a crop—some thirty, some sixty, some a hundred times what was sown."

A lamp on a stand

[21]He said to them, "Do you bring in a lamp to put it under a bowl or a bed? Instead, don't you put it on its stand? [22]For whatever is hidden is meant to be disclosed, and whatever is concealed is meant to be brought out into the open. [23]If anyone has ears to hear, let them hear."

[24]"Consider carefully what you hear," he continued. "With the measure you use, it will be measured to you—and even more. [25]Those who have will be given more; as for those who do not have, even what they have will be taken from them."

The parable of the growing seed

[26]He also said, "This is what the kingdom of God is like. A man scatters seed on the ground. [27]Night and day, whether he sleeps or gets up, the seed sprouts and grows, though he does not know how. [28]All by itself the soil produces corn—first the stalk, then the ear, then the full grain in the ear. [29]As soon as the grain is ripe, he puts the sickle to it, because the harvest has come."

The parable of the mustard seed

[30]Again he said, "What shall we say the kingdom of God is like, or what parable shall we use to describe it? [31]It is like a mustard seed, which is the smallest of all seeds on earth. [32]Yet when planted, it grows and becomes the largest of all

garden plants, with such big branches that the birds can perch in its shade."

³³With many similar parables Jesus spoke the word to them, as much as they could understand. ³⁴He did not say anything to them without using a parable. But when he was alone with his own disciples, he explained everything.

Jesus calms the storm

³⁵That day when evening came, he said to his disciples, "Let us go over to the other side." ³⁶Leaving the crowd behind, they took him along, just as he was, in the boat. There were also other boats with him. ³⁷A furious squall came up, and the waves broke over the boat, so that it was nearly swamped. ³⁸Jesus was in the stern, sleeping on a cushion. The disciples woke him and said to him, "Teacher, don't you care if we drown?"

³⁹He got up, rebuked the wind and said to the waves, "Quiet! Be still!" Then the wind died down and it was completely calm.

⁴⁰He said to his disciples, "Why are you so afraid? Do you still have no faith?"

⁴¹They were terrified and asked each other, "Who is this? Even the wind and the waves obey him!"

Jesus restores a demon-possessed man

5 They went across the lake to the region of the Gerasenes. ²When Jesus got out of the boat, a man with an evil spirit came from the tombs to meet him. ³This man lived in the tombs, and no-one could bind him anymore, not even with a chain. ⁴For he had often been chained hand and

foot, but he tore the chains apart and broke the irons on his feet. No-one was strong enough to subdue him. ⁵Night and day among the tombs and in the hills he would cry out and cut himself with stones.

⁶When he saw Jesus from a distance, he ran and fell on his knees in front of him. ⁷He shouted at the top of his voice, "What do you want with me, Jesus, Son of the Most High God? In God's name don't torture me!" ⁸For Jesus had said to him, "Come out of this man, you evil spirit!"

⁹Then Jesus asked him, "What is your name?"

"My name is Legion," he replied, "for we are many." ¹⁰And he begged Jesus again and again not to send them out of the area.

¹¹A large herd of pigs was feeding on the nearby hillside. ¹²The demons begged Jesus, "Send us among the pigs; allow us to go into them." ¹³He gave them permission, and the evil spirits came out and went into the pigs. The herd, about two thousand in number, rushed down the steep bank into the lake and were drowned.

¹⁴Those tending the pigs ran off and reported this in the town and countryside, and the people went out to see what had happened. ¹⁵When they came to Jesus, they saw the man who had been possessed by the legion of demons, sitting there, dressed and in his right mind; and they were afraid. ¹⁶Those who had seen it told the people what had happened to the demon-possessed man—and told about the pigs as well. ¹⁷Then the people began to plead with Jesus to leave their region.

¹⁸As Jesus was getting into the boat, the man who had been demon-possessed begged to go with him. ¹⁹Jesus did

not let him, but said, "Go home to your own people and tell them how much the Lord has done for you, and how he has had mercy on you." ²⁰So the man went away and began to tell in the Decapolis how much Jesus had done for him. And all the people were amazed.

Jesus raises a dead girl and heals a sick woman

²¹When Jesus had again crossed over by boat to the other side of the lake, a large crowd gathered round him while he was by the lake. ²²Then one of the synagogue leaders, named Jairus, came, and when he saw Jesus, he fell at his feet. ²³He pleaded earnestly with him, "My little daughter is dying. Please come and put your hands on her so that she will be healed and live." ²⁴So Jesus went with him.

A large crowd followed and pressed round him. ²⁵And a woman was there who had been subject to bleeding for twelve years. ²⁶She had suffered a great deal under the care of many doctors and had spent all she had, yet instead of getting better she grew worse. ²⁷When she heard about Jesus, she came up behind him in the crowd and touched his cloak, ²⁸because she thought, "If I just touch his clothes, I will be healed." ²⁹Immediately her bleeding stopped and she felt in her body that she was freed from her suffering.

³⁰At once Jesus realised that power had gone out from him. He turned round in the crowd and asked, "Who touched my clothes?"

³¹"You see the people crowding against you," his disciples answered, "and yet you can ask, 'Who touched me?'"

³²But Jesus kept looking around to see who had done it. ³³Then the woman, knowing what had happened to her, came and fell at his feet and, trembling with fear, told him the whole truth. ³⁴He said to her, "Daughter, your faith has healed you. Go in peace and be freed from your suffering."

³⁵While Jesus was still speaking, some people came from the house of Jairus, the synagogue leader. "Your daughter is dead," they said. "Why bother the teacher anymore?"

³⁶Overhearing what they said, Jesus told him, "Don't be afraid; just believe."

³⁷He did not let anyone follow him except Peter, James and John the brother of James. ³⁸When they came to the home of the synagogue leader, Jesus saw a commotion, with people crying and wailing loudly. ³⁹He went in and said to them, "Why all this commotion and wailing? The child is not dead but asleep." ⁴⁰But they laughed at him.

After he put them all out, he took the child's father and mother and the disciples who were with him, and went in where the child was. ⁴¹He took her by the hand and said to her, *"Talitha koum!"* (which means, "Little girl, I say to you, get up!"). ⁴²Immediately the girl stood up and began to walk around (she was twelve years old). At this they were completely astonished. ⁴³He gave strict orders not to let anyone know about this, and told them to give her something to eat.

A prophet without honour

6 Jesus left there and went to his home town, accompanied by his disciples. ²When the Sabbath came, he began to teach in the synagogue, and many who heard him were amazed.

"Where did this man get these things?" they asked. "What's this wisdom that has been given him? What are these remarkable miracles he is performing? ³Isn't this the carpenter? Isn't this Mary's son and the brother of James, Joseph, Judas and Simon? Aren't his sisters here with us?" And they took offence at him.

⁴Jesus said to them, "Only in their own towns, among their relatives and in their own homes are prophets without honour." ⁵He could not do any miracles there, except lay his hands on a few people who were ill and heal them. ⁶He was amazed at their lack of faith.

Jesus sends out the twelve

Then Jesus went around teaching from village to village. ⁷Calling the Twelve to him, he began to send them out two by two and gave them authority over evil spirits.

⁸These were his instructions: "Take nothing for the journey except a staff—no bread, no bag, no money in your belts. ⁹Wear sandals but not an extra shirt. ¹⁰Whenever you enter a house, stay there until you leave that town. ¹¹And if any place will not welcome you or listen to you, shake the dust off your feet when you leave, as a testimony against them."

¹²They went out and preached that people should repent. ¹³They drove out many demons and anointed with oil many people who were ill and healed them.

John the Baptist beheaded

¹⁴King Herod heard about this, for Jesus' name had

become well known. Some were saying, "John the Baptist has been raised from the dead, and that is why miraculous powers are at work in him."

15Others said, "He is Elijah."

And still others claimed, "He is a prophet, like one of the prophets of long ago."

16But when Herod heard this, he said, "John, whom I beheaded, has been raised from the dead!"

17For Herod himself had given orders to have John arrested, and he had him bound and put in prison. He did this because of Herodias, his brother Philip's wife, whom he had married. 18For John had been saying to Herod, "It is not lawful for you to have your brother's wife." 19So Herodias nursed a grudge against John and wanted to kill him. But she was not able to, 20because Herod feared John and protected him, knowing him to be a righteous and holy man. When Herod heard John, he was greatly puzzled; yet he liked to listen to him.

21Finally the opportune time came. On his birthday Herod gave a banquet for his high officials and military commanders and the leading men of Galilee. 22When the daughter of Herodias came in and danced, she pleased Herod and his dinner guests.

The king said to the girl, "Ask me for anything you want, and I'll give it to you." 23And he promised her with an oath, "Whatever you ask I will give you, up to half my kingdom."

24She went out and said to her mother, "What shall I ask for?"

"The head of John the Baptist," she answered.

25At once the girl hurried in to the king with the request:

"I want you to give me right now the head of John the Baptist on a platter."

26The king was greatly distressed, but because of his oaths and his dinner guests, he did not want to refuse her. 27So he immediately sent an executioner with orders to bring John's head. The man went, beheaded John in the prison, 28and brought back his head on a platter. He presented it to the girl, and she gave it to her mother. 29On hearing of this, John's disciples came and took his body and laid it in a tomb.

Jesus feeds the five thousand

30The apostles gathered round Jesus and reported to him all they had done and taught. 31Then, because so many people were coming and going that they did not even have a chance to eat, he said to them, "Come with me by yourselves to a quiet place and get some rest."

32So they went away by themselves in a boat to a solitary place. 33But many who saw them leaving recognised them and ran on foot from all the towns and got there ahead of them. 34When Jesus landed and saw a large crowd, he had compassion on them, because they were like sheep without a shepherd. So he began teaching them many things.

35By this time it was late in the day, so his disciples came to him. "This is a remote place," they said, "and it's already very late. 36Send the people away so that they can go to the surrounding countryside and villages and buy themselves something to eat."

37But he answered, "You give them something to eat."

They said to him, "That would take eight months of a

man's wages! Are we to go and spend that much on bread and give it to them to eat?"

³⁸"How many loaves do you have?" he asked. "Go and see."

When they found out, they said, "Five – and two fish."

³⁹Then Jesus told them to make all the people sit down in groups on the green grass. ⁴⁰So they sat down in groups of hundreds and fifties. ⁴¹Taking the five loaves and the two fish and looking up to heaven, he gave thanks and broke the loaves. Then he gave them to his disciples to set before the people. He also divided the two fish among them all. ⁴²They all ate and were satisfied, ⁴³and the disciples picked up twelve basketfuls of broken pieces of bread and fish. ⁴⁴The number of the men who had eaten was five thousand.

Jesus walks on the water

⁴⁵Immediately Jesus made his disciples get into the boat and go on ahead of him to Bethsaida, while he dismissed the crowd. ⁴⁶After leaving them, he went up on a mountainside to pray.

⁴⁷When evening came, the boat was in the middle of the lake, and he was alone on land. ⁴⁸He saw the disciples straining at the oars, because the wind was against them. Shortly before dawn he went out to them, walking on the lake. He was about to pass by them, ⁴⁹but when they saw him walking on the lake, they thought he was a ghost. They cried out, ⁵⁰because they all saw him and were terrified.

Immediately he spoke to them and said, "Take courage! It is I. Don't be afraid." ⁵¹Then he climbed into the boat with them, and the wind died down. They were completely amazed, [52]for they had not understood about the loaves; their hearts were hardened.

[53]When they had crossed over, they landed at Gennesaret and anchored there. [54]As soon as they got out of the boat, people recognised Jesus. [55]They ran throughout that whole region and carried those who were ill on mats to wherever they heard he was. [56]And wherever he went—into villages, towns or countryside—they placed those who were ill in the market-places. They begged him to let them touch even the edge of his cloak, and all who touched him were healed.

That which defiles you

7 The Pharisees and some of the teachers of the law who had come from Jerusalem gathered round Jesus [2]and saw some of his disciples eating food with hands that were defiled, that is, unwashed. [3](The Pharisees and all the Jews do not eat unless they give their hands a ceremonial washing, holding to the tradition of the elders. [4]When they come from the market-place they do not eat unless they wash. And they observe many other traditions, such as the washing of cups, pitchers and kettles.)

[5]So the Pharisees and teachers of the law asked Jesus, "Why don't your disciples live according to the tradition of the elders instead of eating their food with defiled hands?"

[6]He replied, "Isaiah was right when he prophesied about you hypocrites; as it is written:

" 'These people honour me with their lips,
    but their hearts are far from me.
[7]They worship me in vain; their teachings are merely
    human rules.' (Isaiah 29.13)

8You have let go of the commands of God and are holding on to human traditions."

9And he continued, "You have a fine way of setting aside the commands of God in order to observe your own traditions! 10For Moses said, 'Honour your father and your mother,' (Exodus 20.12; Deuteronomy 5.16) and, 'Anyone who curses their father or mother must be put to death.' (Exodus 2.17; Leviticus 20.9) 11But you say that if anyone declares that what might have been used to help their father or mother is Corban (that is, devoted to God)—12then you no longer let them do anything for their father or mother. 13Thus you nullify the word of God by your tradition that you have handed down. And you do many things like that."

14Again Jesus called the crowd to him and said, "Listen to me, everyone, and understand this. 15[16]Nothing outside you can defile you by going into you. Rather, it is what comes out of you that defiles you."

17After he had left the crowd and entered the house, his disciples asked him about this parable. 18"Are you so dull?" he asked. "Don't you see that nothing that enters you from the outside can defile you? 19For it doesn't go into your heart but into your stomach, and then out of your body." (In saying this, Jesus declared all foods clean.)

20He went on: "What comes out of you is what defiles you. 21For from within, out of your hearts, come evil thoughts, sexual immorality, theft, murder, 22adultery, greed, malice, deceit, lewdness, envy, slander, arrogance and folly. 23All these evils come from inside and defile you."

Jesus honours a Syro-Phoenician woman's faith

24Jesus left that place and went to the vicinity of Tyre. He entered a house and did not want anyone to know it; yet he could not keep his presence secret. 25In fact, as soon as she heard about him, a woman whose little daughter was possessed by an evil spirit came and fell at his feet. 26The woman was a Greek, born in Syrian Phoenicia. She begged Jesus to drive the demon out of her daughter.

27"First let the children eat all they want," he told her, "for it is not right to take the children's bread and toss it to the dogs."

28"Lord," she replied, "even the dogs under the table eat the children's crumbs."

29Then he told her, "For such a reply, you may go; the demon has left your daughter."

30She went home and found her child lying on the bed, and the demon gone.

Jesus heals a deaf and mute man

31Then Jesus left the vicinity of Tyre and went through Sidon, down to the Sea of Galilee and into the region of the Decapolis. 32There some people brought to him a man who was deaf and could hardly talk, and they begged Jesus to place his hand on him.

33After he took him aside, away from the crowd, Jesus put his fingers into the man's ears. Then he spat and touched the man's tongue. 34He looked up to heaven and with a deep sigh said to him, *"Ephphatha!"* (which means, "Be opened!"). 35At this, the man's ears were opened, his tongue was loosed and he began to speak plainly.

36Jesus commanded them not to tell anyone. But the more he did so, the more they kept talking about it. 37People were overwhelmed with amazement. "He has done everything well," they said. "He even makes the deaf hear and the mute speak."

Jesus feeds the four thousand

8During those days another large crowd gathered. Since they had nothing to eat, Jesus called his disciples to him and said, 2"I have compassion for these people; they have already been with me three days and have nothing to eat. 3If I send them home hungry, they will collapse on the way, because some of them have come a long distance."

4His disciples answered, "But where in this remote place can anyone get enough bread to feed them?"

5"How many loaves do you have?" Jesus asked.

"Seven," they replied.

6He told the crowd to sit down on the ground. When he had taken the seven loaves and given thanks, he broke them and gave them to his disciples to set before the people, and they did so. 7They had a few small fish as well; he gave thanks for them also and told the disciples to distribute them. 8The people ate and were satisfied. Afterwards the disciples picked up seven basketfuls of broken pieces that were left over. 9About four thousand were present. And having sent them away, 10he got into the boat with his disciples and went to the region of Dalmanutha.

11The Pharisees came and began to question Jesus. To test him, they asked him for a sign from heaven. 12He sighed deeply and said, "Why does this generation ask for a sign?

Truly I tell you, no sign will be given to it." [13]Then he left them, got back into the boat and crossed to the other side.

The yeast of the Pharisees and Herod

[14]The disciples had forgotten to bring bread, except for one loaf they had with them in the boat. [15]"Be careful," Jesus warned them. "Watch out for the yeast of the Pharisees and that of Herod."

[16]They discussed this with one another and said, "It is because we have no bread."

[17]Aware of their discussion, Jesus asked them: "Why are you talking about having no bread? Do you still not see or understand? Are your hearts hardened? [18]Do you have eyes but fail to see, and ears but fail to hear? And don't you remember? [19]When I broke the five loaves for the five thousand, how many basketfuls of pieces did you pick up?"

"Twelve," they replied.

[20]"And when I broke the seven loaves for the four thousand, how many basketfuls of pieces did you pick up?"

They answered, "Seven."

[21]He said to them, "Do you still not understand?"

Jesus heals a blind man at Bethsaida

[22]They came to Bethsaida, and some people brought a blind man and begged Jesus to touch him. [23]He took the blind man by the hand and led him outside the village. When he had spat on the man's eyes and put his hands on him, Jesus asked, "Do you see anything?"

[24]He looked up and said, "I see people; they look like trees walking around."

²⁵Once more Jesus put his hands on the man's eyes. Then his eyes were opened, his sight was restored, and he saw everything clearly. ²⁶Jesus sent him home, saying, "Don't even go into the village.

Peter declares that Jesus is the Messiah

²⁷Jesus and his disciples went on to the villages around Caesarea Philippi. On the way he asked them, "Who do people say I am?"

²⁸They replied, "Some say John the Baptist; others say Elijah; and still others, one of the prophets."

²⁹"But what about you?" he asked. "Who do you say I am?"

Peter answered, "You are the Messiah."

³⁰Jesus warned them not to tell anyone about him.

[continued on page 79]

You probably noticed Jesus trying to keep it quiet by asking people not to talk about him, preventing evil spirits declaring his identity and teaching in parables so that the meaning of what he was saying was not immediately apparent. The truth about Jesus will be revealed at the right time. Supremely the final revelation of Jesus' identity takes place in the events of his death and resurrection. Jesus' teaching can only be properly understood in the light of the cross.

The way the story unfolds in the gospel becomes much clearer from the perspective of what happens at the end. In the movie 'The Sixth Sense' Bruce Willis plays a child psychologist who helps a young boy who sees dead people. The film comes to a surprising denouement when we discover that the Willis character is in fact dead. The immediate reaction is to want to watch the movie again. From the perspective of what happens at the end you see things differently and appreciate the intention of the storyteller. As you read the gospel you will notice many things but they only really start to fall into place from the perspective that you get at the end.

I shouldn't say any more in case I spoil it for you (especially since I may have just ruined your enjoyment of "The Sixth Sense"!).

The time has come

After John was imprisoned Jesus proclaimed, 'The time has come' (Mark 1.15).

We do not know why this was the chosen time. Different theories have been articulated as to why this may have been the selected hour. Some speculate that communication was facilitated by the might of the Roman Empire its roads, its common language, its trading links and its peace. In truth we have no idea. What we do know is that it was God's time. God chooses to intervene in this way at this time in human history. God is sovereign over the affairs of nations and of humanity. We may wonder, 'why now?', but the more important concern is, 'so what?' God may choose to speak to you at a particular time in your life. That is his prerogative – are you listening and what are you going to do about it?

Jesus makes a public statement 'The kingdom of God has come near. Repent and believe the good news!' (Mark 1.15). He continues John's theme of repentance but ties it in with the announcement of the kingdom of God. Jesus is going to mention the kingdom of God fourteen times in Mark's

Gospel and over a hundred times between all four gospels. A kingdom by definition is ruled by a king. Many of Jesus contemporaries misunderstood what he was saying when he spoke about his kingdom – they assumed that he was going to lead a popular uprising against the Roman invaders and restore the government of the land to God's chosen ruler. They looked back to the kingdoms of David and Solomon as the golden era in their history and longed for God to bring back that kind of arrangement. The prophecy that God would raise up a king to rule on David's throne forever was understood by them to mean a political appointment.

The kingdom that Jesus is speaking of is quite different. Citizenship of this new kingdom is by choice not by birth, the boundaries of this kingdom are global not national and the glories of this kingdom are future not past. Jesus, when questioned by the Pharisees about the kingdom, answered, 'that the kingdom of God is within you' (Luke 17.21). Jesus tells Pilate that he is a king but that 'my kingdom is not of this world' (John 18.36). Paul in his letter to the Romans explains, 'the kingdom of God is … a matter of … righteousness, peace and joy in the Holy Spirit' (Romans 14.17). The kingdom looked forward to by the prophets starts in the hearts and lives of those who acknowledge him as king but there is more to be looked forward to. We will see later that the kingdom has a huge future dimension and that our place in that depends on our response in the present.

Do you want a chance to change the world?
Jesus calls Peter and Andrew to follow him (Mark 1.16). The change of direction called for becomes clearer. It is turning

from sins and turning *to* Jesus. Peter and Andrew probably had no idea what it was going to mean to be a fisher of men apart from the possible thought that you might need pretty big nets. What they do realize is that they are being invited to follow Jesus and to embark on something of great significance.

When Steve Jobs started Apple Computers, it seemed to most people that the PC industry would always be a marginal business. Thomas Watson, chairman of IBM in 1943 said, 'I think there is a world market for maybe five computers.' As late as 1977 Ken Olsen, president, chairman and founder of Digital Equipment Corporation, opined 'There is no reason for any individual to have a computer in their home.' Jobs thought otherwise and he knew he needed a business genius. Surveying the market he approached someone at the pinnacle of his profession. His chosen target was Pepsi CEO John Sculley. In 1983 he made his pitch but was very politely turned down. Jobs eventually posed a famous question that was to get him his man. 'Do you want to spend the rest of your life selling sugared water or do you want a chance to change the world?'

Jesus did something more remarkable still. He took ordinary men, probably in their late teens and early twenties, and used them to change the world. Accepting the invitation was not without cost; they left their trade and professional livelihoods and followed him. They gave up their security and what mattered to them most and embarked on this new adventure with Jesus.

For James and John the response was just as immediate but the relational cost is also emphasized; they left their father. What moved these young men to give up what they held most dear and go with Jesus? There was clearly something about him, something about the kingdom, something about his call, something that they determined not to miss out on.

Another dimension

Harry Potter lives an everyday sort of existence until he discovers that there is a whole world that had been previously unknown to him. Hagrid takes him to Gringotts Bank run by goblins, a secret street, Diagon Alley and the now famous Hogwarts Express from platform 9¾ which introduce him to a whole new dimension. It is easy to accept the premise in a children's book that there might be other dimensions to life but harder when it comes to real life. J.K. Rowling was writing fiction, Mark is writing fact but some of the things he writes about seem more at home in the world of Harry Potter or Tolkien. We have a great attachment in western culture to secular materialism; many of us view talk of evil spirits, demons, angels and the devil as mythology left over from a less enlightened era. The Bible is quite specific that there is a spiritual realm where a battle wages between good and evil. Evil is not an impersonal force but a personality. The Devil and his forces are utterly opposed to God and are hell bent on distorting his nature and preventing people from responding to his word.

One Sabbath day Jesus was preaching in the synagogue in Capernaum (Mark 1.21). The congregation was amazed because he taught in a way that was different from anything they had heard before. Jesus was not like the teachers of the law – he spoke with authority. As he was speaking a man in the synagogue cried out. The man was possessed by an evil spirit who had also heard and recognized the voice of authority. 'We know who you are', it shouted, 'the Holy One of God' (Mark 1.24). Jesus silenced the spirit, which was subject to his authority. The spirit shook the man and fled his body. The man was delivered and Mark uses the same word as earlier to describe the crowd's reaction – amazement (Mark 1.27). News about Jesus spread quickly throughout Galilee. Here was someone who had authority in the world and over spirits. The whole town assembled as the buzz about what had happened spread like wildfire.

Jesus travelled through the region preaching in synagogues, healed many different diseases and cast out evil spirits. We see in the episode at Capernaum that it is the preaching which produces the response from the demons. Jesus is pushing back the influence of the powers of darkness as he preaches and teaches and as he heals the sick and delivers the possessed.

Taking the roof off

Jesus travelled back to Capernaum (Mark 2.1). Hardly surprisingly there was a huge crowd. The building and the area around the door were packed solid with people. Four friends arrived carrying one of their mates on a stretcher. Perhaps he was heavier than they thought, perhaps they set out late, or perhaps they underestimated the demand – but when they got there, it was a capacity crowd. They couldn't get anywhere near. But instead of giving up and going home, these resourceful guys hatched a cunning plan. They hauled the stretcher up onto the flat roof of the building and began making a hole. The paralysed man was lucky to have friends with this kind of commitment! They really believed that Jesus could do something for him. You can imagine people inside wondering what on earth was going on as pieces of the ceiling fell to the floor and then the sky became visible. As the hole got larger and larger curious faces peered in and then to everybody's surprise a mat bearing the paralytic is lowered slowly through the roof, to the floor, arriving right in front of Jesus. Jesus sees their faith and speaks to the man with surprising words, 'son your sins are forgiven' (v. 5).

This was not what the friends or the crowd were expecting. Some of the theologians present started thinking to themselves, 'He's taken that too far! Only God can forgive sins'. They had been interested to observe the healings and hear the teaching but now they concluded this was blasphemy. Jesus knew exactly what they were thinking and went ballistic. Jesus reserved this kind of outburst exclusively for religious teachers and leaders. 'Which is easier: to say to this paralysed man, "Your sins are forgiven," or to say, "Get up, take your mat and walk"?' The man is healed by Jesus and walks home with his mobility restored *and* his sins forgiven. It must have been a squeeze for the crowd pushing back to make space for him to leave!

Jesus states, 'The Son of Man has authority on earth to forgive sins'. 'Son of Man' is the title Jesus uses most frequently to talk about himself. In the book of Daniel, written centuries before, a figure called the son of man is described.

In my vision at night I looked, and there before me was one like a son of man, coming with the clouds of heaven. He approached the Ancient of Days and was led into his presence. He was given authority, glory and sovereign power; all peoples, nations and men of every language worshipped him. His dominion is an everlasting dominion that will not pass away, and his kingdom is one that will never be destroyed. (Daniel 7.13–14)

These verses refer to two characters: the 'Ancient of Days', which is a title of God used elsewhere in the book of Daniel, and 'one like a son of man'. This figure with human characteristics is given authority and sovereign power, is worshipped by all nations and is the king of a kingdom which will last forever.

Even in the episodes we have looked at so far we can begin to see why Jesus is using this title in a messianic way.

Mark again uses the only word he can think of to describe the reaction – amazement. Everyone praises God saying they have never seen anything like this!

Whose side are you on?

From this point on there is increased opposition to Jesus from the Pharisees, an influential enclave within the religious establishment. They are jealous of his popularity, critical of his association with tax gatherers and sinners, aggrieved by his disciple's non-observance of fasting and angered by his attitude to the Sabbath (see Mark 2.16, 2.18 and 2.23–24). They are consistently against Jesus at every turn. At the start of Chapter 3 there is an incident in an unnamed synagogue where Jesus heals a man with a withered hand. Again the Pharisees object and Jesus is angry and distressed at their hard and stubborn hearts. Over a period of time they have taken a look at Jesus, questioned him, then challenged him – now the opposition steps up a gear. The

Pharisees and the Herodians hatch a conspiracy. The supporters of the puppet King Herod, kept in place by the Romans and the Pharisees, start to plot how they are going to assassinate Jesus. Political and religious power unite in an unholy alliance to plan to get rid of Jesus. Having accused Jesus of breaking their interpretation of various command-ments they are now ready to break God's law and civil law. The hypocrisy is breathtaking.

I recall reading an article after the death at an early age of the actor River Phoenix. He had spoken publicly against drugs and died of an overdose. The column concluded with a telling comment that has stuck with me – 'Old habits die hard and hypocrisy is eternal.' Later in the Gospel of Mark (ch. 8), Jesus warns the disciples to beware the yeast of the Pharisees, to take care that hardness of heart and hypocrisy do not infect their lives. Hypocrisy among church leaders who have publicly asserted one thing and privately lived another has been a major factor in turning people away from Jesus. You may have had a negative experience yourself. I am sorry if that has been the case and confess there are things in my life that would not be the best advert for the Christian faith. But I hope you will make your judgment based on Jesus.

There is a final judgment coming which you and I will have to face. Right now we are on one side or another in this conflict. We are either for Jesus or against him. Whose side are you on?

How is your heart condition?
News about Jesus was spreading fast. Large crowds were gath-ering to see for themselves this man who healed the sick, who

cast out demons and who taught with authority. Jesus was becoming the celebrity phenomenon of his day. Everywhere that he went people gathered, crowding round to get close. At the start of Mark 4 Jesus begins to teach by the shore of Lake Galilee and has to relocate to a boat as a platform for safe and effective communication. Jesus often taught in 'parables'. These were memorable stories used to illustrate a spiritual truth. Usually an example is taken from everyday life and applied in a new and surprising way. They are short tales of the unexpected, often making a single key point. Jesus chose this method of communication to engage with ordinary people but also to hide the full and immediate impact of his teaching. He taught in parables so that people would listen to what he was saying and reflect on it but the full meaning would only become clear later.

For example, in the parable of the sower, Mark (ch. 4) records for us the story and also a private explanation of its meaning given to the disciples later. The story is an agricultural one. A farmer sows seed, not in neat little drills in but in handfuls over mixed terrain. What happens is pretty much what would be expected. The seed lands in different environments and a variety of reactions take place. Birds peck the seed on the hard, compacted path. The seed in the rocky ground takes root but in the shallow soil there is no depth to the roots and, although initially the signs are promising, when the heat is on the plants wilt and die. Some seed falls among the weeds and again, although initial growth is vigorous, it is strangled by the competition. The seed that falls on the good soil produces a harvest but what is described is a remarkably fruitful harvest. This emphasis on fruitfulness way beyond what the listeners would have expected is the sting in the tail of this parable. Some of the seed produces a harvest of Jack-and-the-beanstalk proportions, not in height but in yield. In the good soil there is a bumper return – in the other types of soil there is none.

Jesus tells this parable at the height of his human popularity. He is not fooled by people's interest; he knows what they are really like. This is an important distinction between the way we judge people and the way that God judges them. We look on the outside but God looks on the heart.

Afterwards Jesus explains the parable to his disciples and draws a comparison between the types of soil and different types of people. This is not a personality evaluation or a self-assessment exercise. People's response to the word of God reveals what kind of soil they are like. The path represents those who hear the word but the devil snatches it away. This is another glimpse into the reality of conflict in the spiritual realm; Satan does not want people to receive God's word. The rocky places are like people who respond enthusiastically but can't hack it when persecution or opposition comes. The weeds represent the worries of life and the desire for money and material things. It is not possible to love God and money; it is incongruous to trust God and worry. A preoccupation with possessions, power and position leads to an inevitable fruitlessness.

The good soil stands for those who hear and accept God's word. In them it multiplies and produces a great harvest. This is stark stuff. What counts with God is not so much reputation, effort, morality or charity – rather it is response to his word. How do you respond to God's word? What kind of soil do you think you are most like? God knows.

Gerrard Jones is reading Maths, at St Hugh's College, Oxford.

I come from a non-Christian home, but I have always believed in a God and in life after death. In summer 2000, I was worried about my A-level results, and getting into Oxford. So I prayed to my God, and made an 'agreement' with him, that if he gave me the grades I needed then I would read the Bible.

Before I read it I thought that I knew God and that he was very pleased with me because I was a nice person who tried hard. But when I started reading it, I realized that it didn't say that at all. In fact he seemed to deal quite harshly with people like me, who ignored his requirements. But I read through it too fast, and managed to miss the main point of the New Testament ...

God did give me the grades to come to Oxford, and part of my 'agreement' was to start going to church. When I did it was a surprise! The preacher was saying that if I didn't know Christ then my relationship with God was not right. This started to worry me, that God would be angry with me. Eventually, a Christian friend offered to explain the gospel to me over dinner, and I took him up on this.

When I heard exactly what Jesus had said and taught, I realized that I didn't really know him. But he knew me, and everything that was in my heart. I knew that if a man who lived 2000 years ago could know this then he must be God.

So that night I prayed to God, saying that I was truly sorry for going against him and asked for forgiveness through Jesus. I felt as though a great weight was lifted from my back, and I still have that joy and peace.

Perfect storm

I enjoy messing about in boats. One of the best months for our family was living on a small island off the west coast of Canada. We had the use of a canoe and a whaler and really enjoyed exploring the area. The more time you spend on the water the more you develop a healthy respect for the sea. It is frightening how quickly the wind can pick up and the weather can turn. An idyllic situation can turn to potential danger. I remember speaking in Canada to a fisherman who had lost his closest friend and his son when their boat got caught in a storm. One of his comments was quite haunting: 'I am always aware that the place where I work could become my grave.'

The disciples were a mixed group. Some of them had grown up in fishing families and worked for years on boats, others were landlubbers. You can imagine their feelings as the weather starts to change (Mark 4.35–37) – a gnawing concern, giving way to a growing concern as the situation worsens. The increasing intensity of the storm brings anxiety and ultimately panic as even the hardened fishermen struggle to keep the bow straight into the wind. The situation is getting desperate. The waves are breaking over the boat and the boat is filling faster than they can bale. This is 'Goodnight Capernaum' as far as they are concerned and they are terrified. Most frustratingly of all Jesus is sleeping in the back on a cushion. As a last resort they wake Jesus and ask if he cares that they are going to drown. They could have woken him earlier but they only turn to him as a last resort. The question 'Teacher don't you care?' is almost rhetorical – it seems that nothing can be done. Jesus speaks into the chaotic situation. He addresses the storm, telling it to be still. Instantly things are transformed – the choppy sea becomes a millpond, the wind is silenced.

The disciples are rebuked for their fear and lack of faith

They are amazed at what has happened and ask each other, 'Who is this that the wind and waves obey him?' They have addressed him as teacher but clearly that is not a sufficient explanation for what they have just experienced together. They do not know what to make of it. There is only one person whose word has the authority to elicit this kind of response.

God reveals himself in the Bible as the God who speaks and there is power in his word. In the Genesis account of the beginning of the universe God creates through his spoken word. God speaks through the Old Testament, making promises, establishing a binding relationship of covenant, giving law and calling to repentance. Jesus is described at the start of John's Gospel as 'The Word' who was with God in the beginning. The Word of God makes the critical difference in the midst of the storm. God's Word can bring peace to the confusion of our lives and will bring order to the chaos of the world. Only God can do this. If only we would not be so independent, so hard of heart and so slow to call on him to intervene – what a difference that could make!

Pigs can't fly

In the region of the Gerasenes Jesus encountered a very disturbed individual (see Mark 5). This man lived in the tombs isolated from human contact. He would cry continually and cut himself with stones. Attempts had been made to restrain him but to no avail; he had snapped every cord used to bind him, even chains. This is the result of demon possession. It is farcical to consider the accusations of the Pharisees at some points that Jesus is demon possessed when you look at what real demon possession is like. Jesus brings people into community, heals and values them whereas demonic activity drives people to the margins of society, harms and exploits them. Rebellion against God in all its forms is destructive to human life and relationships.

When Jesus arrives the man comes rushing to meet him. He addresses Jesus as Son of the Most High God and begs not to be tortured. One of the lies of the evil one is that God is going to make things worse and do you more harm; nothing is further from the truth. The man tells Jesus that his name is Legion and begs him again not to send the demons away. There is resistance to the one thing which can change his circumstances. Sometimes 'the devil we know' can seem more attractive but Jesus knows better and sees beyond the protestations. At this point the demons read the writing on the wall and ask to be sent into a herd of pigs nearby. The demons enter the pigs and they rush down a precipice into the lake. The herd of pigs is destroyed and the man is delivered, again demonstrating the opposite agenda of God and the Devil.

Later, the crowd see the man clothed and in his right mind. The contrast between before and after must have been a massive shock. This is no cosmetic makeover – this is a total transformation. The crowd is afraid and pleads with Jesus to leave. The man wants to go with Jesus but is encouraged to go home and tell his family and friends about the Lord's mercy. He travels through the ten-city area (the 'Decapolis', Mark 5.20) talking about what Jesus has done for him. Mark uses his favourite word to describe the people's reaction – they are amazed.

Talitha koum

Back on his usual side of the lake, Jesus was met by a synagogue leader named Jairus (Mark 5.21–43). Jairus was really worried about his daughter who was at death's door. He had probably been waiting for Jesus to come back, pacing the shoreline, growing increasingly frantic with every passing hour. Although a man of standing in the community he is so desperate that he falls at Jesus' feet and begs him to come and lay hands on his daughter and heal her. Any parent will readily identify with the emotion and urgency in the situation. Jesus goes with him. As they are walking a woman with a serious medical condition sees her opportunity.

She has suffered from bleeding for twelve years and has virtually bankrupted herself on doctors' fees trying to find a cure. She figures if she could just touch Jesus' clothes she would be healed. She does so and immediately her bleeding stops and she senses she is healed. Jesus turns around and asks who had touched his clothes. It seems a ridiculous question to the disciples, with the thronging crowd pressing in on all sides – a more sensible question would be who *hadn't* touched his clothes. Jesus persists and the woman, knowing what has happened, comes with fear and trembling to Jesus feet. The presence of God without the word of God is a terrifying thing. Jesus wanted to talk to her. Jesus spoke to her, confirming that she had been healed and sent her on her way in peace. God's blessing cannot be stolen – it is given. Jesus' word mediates wholeness, acceptance and peace to the woman.

Just then a messenger arrives with devastating news for Jairus that his daughter is dead and he should not bother Jesus any more. They have been delayed too long and the situation seems now beyond Jesus' power. But Jesus tells Jairus, 'Don't be afraid, only believe'. When they get to the house it is in uproar. He tells them that the child is not dead but only sleeping, which only elicits a cynical laugh. The crowd knew that she was dead. Jesus clears the house of the mourning family, neighbours and friends and leads Jairus and his wife and Peter, James and John into the childs room. Taking the twelve-year-old girl by the hand he says '*Talitha koum*', which means 'little girl, get up' in Aramaic. These two simple words bring her back, to the astonishment of those present. Jesus gives two women beyond the help of medicine new life. A little faith goes a long way.

These last three stories would make a compelling focus for a documentary or a Jerry Springer special. 'People beyond help – saved by Jesus.' These are real life ordinary folks whose lives are totally transformed in a way which significantly impacts their relationships and community. I meet people who tell me that they are beyond God's help, that the choices that they have made and the things which have happened to them mean that God can do nothing for them. This is simply not true. Jesus refreshes the parts nothing else can reach.

The engine room

I have a friend called Simon whom I got to know when he and his wife were exploring joining the church. Ailsa and I did a course with them. (I have changed the name to protect his identity – his real name is Colin.) One of the big issues for Simon was that he couldn't accept the idea that he fell short of God's standards. Simon is a great guy – he works hard, is a good husband and father, he tries to be helpful, honest and kind, and he had even started coming to church on a regular basis. As we chatted this through he started to articulate the notion that while things were mostly all right on the outside, sometimes he was aware of stuff on the inside. He called this the engine room of his life by which he meant the driving force, motivations and attitudes at the core of our beings. We realize that there is a problem in the engine room of our lives when we try to do things under our own steam, when we exclude God and try to do things our own way and when our power to love runs out. The engine room can be in need of an overhaul. True transformation happens when God comes in and begins to change us from the inside out.

A high-powered delegation of Pharisees and religious leaders was sent from Jerusalem to Jesus (see Mark 7). They challenged Jesus about his disciples not following the tradition of ritual washing that would keep their food pure. This was about a religious ritual not a food hygiene thing! Jesus called them hypocrites and quoted from Isaiah. 'These people honour me with their lips but their hearts are far from me.' (Isaiah 29.13). He goes on to explain to the crowd, 'nothing that comes in from outside makes a person unclean – it is what comes out of a person which makes them unclean.'

The problem is internal to the human condition. Someone once said, 'the heart of the human problem is the problem of the human heart.' Jesus spells out exactly what the problem with the engine room is. 'For from within, out of your hearts, come evil thoughts, sexual immorality, theft, murder, adultery, greed, malice, deceit, lewdness, envy, slander, arrogance and folly. All these evils come from inside and defile you.' (Mark 7.21–23) It is quite a list! These things are the symptoms of humanity living in rebellion against God.

Religion is not going to make things any better. Any human solution is doomed to failure because it comes from the same set of basic attitudes and motivations. Human beings are amazing. We are made in the image of God with unique personalities, abilities and capacities. But this image is marred. We might be able to do a little better than the next person by whatever comparative standard we choose to adopt but we will never please God until our hearts are different. This is something we are powerless to change.

I have spent most of my life playing in some sort of sports team. Being men we don't give much away of what is going on inside but occasionally we let our guards slip. Often it happens in the drinking progression somewhere between 'relaxed' and 'everything is funny'. One night at a hockey dinner, Andy told me, 'I am so mucked up, it must be great to have a new start. You're a Christian, how can I be born again?' I was slightly taken aback – it was certainly not language that he had heard me use. 'Andy,' I replied, 'that is a really brilliant question but the tragic thing is, if I tell you the answer you probably won't remember anything about this conversation in the morning'. He giggled, which wasn't a good sign. 'Tell you what,' I said. 'It is such a great question that I am going to write it on your arm so you will know you asked it tomorrow.' I got a marker pen from behind the bar and wrote, 'How can I be born again?' in big letters up his arm. It was funnier at the time than it seems now! The next week we had a laugh about how drunk he must have been but we never spoke seriously about the issue again.

I think many of us blot out the big questions of life, finding ways to escape reality. Sometimes we glimpse that there might be more. The reminders of these moments of clarity are not generally written on the outside of our bodies by strange friends. This is life not *Memento* after all. The clues are inside us, the longing for eternity, wanting acceptance, needing forgiveness, wrestling with conscience, seeking transcendence, yearning for true love and searching for meaning and value.

We are hungry, who can satisfy?

On two occasions in Mark's Gospel Jesus feeds large crowds – one of 5000 and one of 4000 (Mark 6.30–44 and 8.1–21). On both occasions it was a similar story. At the end of a day of teaching and ministry the crowd was hungry and a distance from the nearest place to get food, in the unlikely event there was anywhere in Galilee which did takeaway for that number of folks. On both occasions Jesus dealt with the need by taking a small amount of food, blessing it and distributing it to the crowd. Everyone ate their fill and was satisfied and there were basketfuls of leftovers collected at the end. Jesus' concern is to bless the masses and to show in a tangible way his grace, generosity and sufficiency. These events are not illustrations about the importance of sharing but rather demonstrations of Jesus providing nourishment and sustenance.

The disciples did not grasp why he had done this. They made the mistake of thinking that Jesus was going to deal with peoples felt needs. The problem with felt needs is that they are not always predictive of real need. Much of the time for example we can blind ourselves to the problems of the engine room. Similarly the presenting need may mask a deeper need. A hungry person may for instance have cancer and while a good meal will address one need they have it will not address their fundamental condition. Jesus addresses the root causes of the human condition. The primary need that men and women have is Jesus himself. They may well be unaware of this but it is true. Jesus did not come to provide bread – he came to *be* the bread for people, feeding, nourishing and filling them. In John's Gospel it is the most explicit when Jesus says, 'I am the bread of life. Whoever comes to me will never go hungry, and whoever believes in me will never be thirsty.' (John 6.35)

Jesus satisfies, not by giving us things but by giving us himself.

Identity revealed

Obviously there was considerable public speculation on the subject of Jesus' identity. There was a buzz going round the country and different groups had developed different ideas. The disciples probably got caught up in this, listening to the theories, fielding questions, discussing among themselves what the answer might be. No one really knew.

One day in the vicinity of Caesarea Philippi Jesus engaged

the disciples on this topic (Mark 8.27–30). He asked them a direct question, 'Who do people say I am?' The theories come spilling out. Some favour the Elijah theory, some think one of the prophets, others that John the Baptist has come back to life. What is interesting about this is that no one comes up with an obvious explanation. All the theories offered are supernatural. Naturalistic explanations just will not do. They do not say, 'some say you are a great teacher, others a charismatic leader, others a mystical guru.' He lived close to people and although they could not explain it they knew he was something special. The contemporary experience of those who were there with Jesus pushed them towards an extreme conclusion.

Jesus turns to the disciples and makes it personal. 'But who do you say that I am?' This ups the stakes from general speculation to personal decision. Peter answers using the Greek word for the Hebrew Messiah, 'You are the Christ'. Could Jesus really be the long awaited, promised and prophesied Messiah who would save people from their sins and establish the new kingdom? Some had assumed that this was going to mean political revolution, which is one reason Jesus avoids public proclamation. Others had a clear religious framework, but they were not expecting things to work out like this either.

Jesus begins to help his disciples see how his work is going to be completed. It is going to involve suffering, rejection by the chief priests and teachers of the law, and will culminate in his death and resurrection. All this is too much for Peter – he doesn't want Jesus to die; there must be an alternative strategy. Jesus rebukes him strongly, asserting that Peter is not concerned for the things of God. Jesus has come from God on a rescue mission that is divine in its conception and its implementation.

The plan is not about happiness, popularity, power, wealth or empire – it is to restore relationship with God, to rescue humanity from the dominion of darkness and death and evil and sin. It concerns redemption from the penalty of rebellion against God and salvation from the consequences of that wrath and future judgment. It is an awesome message centred on the cross.

REAL LIVES

Laura Calder is reading History, at Keble College, Oxford.

When I came up to Oxford I didn't have the slightest intention of ever finding myself inside a church. I knew all about Christianity. I believed in God, but would get really stressed whenever I started to think about it, and was forever putting it off until there was more time. I didn't think any particular religion had it completely right, so preferred to pick and mix the bits I liked best. I thought churches brainwashed people, and to be quite honest people talking about being 'saved' always struck me as being a bit dodgy.

Somehow, though, I ended up in an OICCU meeting near the end of my first year. It really took me by surprise. I was completely shocked by the number of students who were there and clearly so passionate about God. Surely there were better things to be doing on a Wednesday night – why weren't they at Park End? Anyway, I continued going along to Church and OICCU things and really enjoyed them.

But I kept on finding that I was always getting stuck on the issue of Jesus. I would have been completely happy in church if they could have just missed him out. I couldn't believe what they were saying. It all came to a head when I realized that I really wasn't worshipping the same God as everyone else, and I needed to work out once and for all whether they were right or not.

I concluded that Jesus was the Son of God, and my whole outlook has completely changed. Since my dad died I'd felt like I was being blown around from one crisis to the next. Every time I'd try and get on with my life I'd be knocked off course again. But now I have such a deep sense of security and peace. Although things still go wrong, I've always got my relationship with God and the promises he's made to me.

From this point in the narrative Jesus talks much more explicitly about his death. He tells the disciples what is going to happen. He is going to be rejected by the chief priests, be put to death and three days later rise again. This section contains three predictions: in 8.31, 9.31 and 10.33. As the pace quickens the action starts to move from Galilee towards Jerusalem where Jesus knows his death awaits him.

[continued from page 55]

MARK 8.31–10.52

Jesus predicts his death

³¹He then began to teach them that the Son of Man must suffer many things and be rejected by the elders, the chief priests and the teachers of the law, and that he must be killed and after three days rise again. ³²He spoke plainly about this, and Peter took him aside and began to rebuke him.

³³But when Jesus turned and looked at his disciples, he rebuked Peter. "Get behind me, Satan!" he said. "You do not have in mind the concerns of God, but merely human concerns."

The way of the cross

³⁴Then he called the crowd to him along with his disciples and said: "Those who would be my disciples must deny themselves and take up their cross and follow me. ³⁵For those who want to save their life will lose it, but those who lose their life for me and for the gospel will save it. ³⁶What good is it for you to gain the whole world, yet forfeit your soul? ³⁷Or what can you give in exchange for your soul? ³⁸If any of you are ashamed of me and my words in this adulterous and sinful generation, the Son of Man will be ashamed of you when he comes in his Father's glory with the holy angels."

9 And he said to them, "Truly I tell you, some who are standing here will not taste death before they see that the kingdom of God has come with power."

The transfiguration

²After six days Jesus took Peter, James and John with him and led them up a high mountain, where they were all alone. There he was transfigured before them. ³His clothes became dazzling white, whiter than anyone in the world could bleach them. ⁴And there appeared before them Elijah and Moses, who were talking with Jesus.

⁵Peter said to Jesus, "Rabbi, it is good for us to be here. Let us put up three shelters—one for you, one for Moses and one for Elijah." ⁶(He did not know what to say, they were so frightened.)

⁷Then a cloud appeared and covered them, and a voice came from the cloud: "This is my Son, whom I love. Listen to him!"

⁸Suddenly, when they looked around, they no longer saw anyone with them except Jesus.

⁹As they were coming down the mountain, Jesus gave them orders not to tell anyone what they had seen until the Son of Man had risen from the dead. ¹⁰They kept the matter to themselves, discussing what "rising from the dead" meant.

¹¹And they asked him, "Why do the teachers of the law say that Elijah must come first?"

¹²Jesus replied, "To be sure, Elijah does come first, and restores all things. Why then is it written that the Son of Man must suffer much and be rejected? ¹³But I tell you, Elijah has come, and they have done to him everything they wished, just as it is written about him."

Jesus heals a demon-possessed boy

¹⁴When they came to the other disciples, they saw a large crowd around them and the teachers of the law arguing with them. ¹⁵As soon as all the people saw Jesus, they were overwhelmed with wonder and ran to greet him.

¹⁶"What are you arguing with them about?" he asked.

¹⁷A man in the crowd answered, "Teacher, I brought you my son, who is possessed by a spirit that has robbed him of speech. ¹⁸Whenever it seizes him, it throws him to the ground. He foams at the mouth, gnashes his teeth and becomes rigid. I asked your disciples to drive out the spirit, but they could not."

¹⁹"You unbelieving generation," Jesus replied, "how long shall I stay with you? How long shall I put up with you? Bring the boy to me."

²⁰So they brought him. When the spirit saw Jesus, it immediately threw the boy into a convulsion. He fell to the ground and rolled around, foaming at the mouth.

²¹Jesus asked the boy's father, "How long has he been like this?"

"From childhood," he answered. ²²"It has often thrown him into fire or water to kill him. But if you can do anything, take pity on us and help us."

²³" 'If you can'?" said Jesus. "Everything is possible for one who believes."

²⁴Immediately the boy's father exclaimed, "I do believe; help me overcome my unbelief!"

²⁵When Jesus saw that a crowd was running to the scene, he rebuked the evil spirit. "You deaf and mute spirit," he said, "I command you, come out of him and never enter him again."

²⁶The spirit shrieked, convulsed him violently and came out. The boy looked so much like a corpse that many said, "He's dead." ²⁷But Jesus took him by the hand and lifted him to his feet, and he stood up.

²⁸After Jesus had gone indoors, his disciples asked him privately, "Why couldn't we drive it out?"

²⁹He replied, "This kind can come out only by prayer."

Jesus predicts his death a second time

³⁰They left that place and passed through Galilee. Jesus did not want anyone to know where they were, ³¹because he was teaching his disciples. He said to them, "The Son of Man is going to be delivered over to human hands. He will be killed, and after three days he will rise." ³²But they did

not understand what he meant and were afraid to ask him about it.

33They came to Capernaum. When he was in the house, he asked them, "What were you arguing about on the road?" 34But they kept quiet because on the way they had argued about who was the greatest.

35Sitting down, Jesus called the Twelve and said, "Anyone who wants to be first must be the very last, and the servant of all."

36He took a little child whom he placed among them. Taking the child in his arms, he said to them, 37"Whoever welcomes one of these little children in my name welcomes me; and whoever welcomes me does not welcome me but the one who sent me."

Whoever is not against us is for us

38"Teacher," said John, "we saw someone driving out demons in your name and we told him to stop, because he was not one of us."

39"Do not stop him," Jesus said. "No-one who does a miracle in my name can in the next moment say anything bad about me, 40for whoever is not against us is for us. 41Truly I tell you, anyone who gives you a cup of water in my name because you belong to the Messiah will certainly be rewarded."

Causing to stumble

42"If anyone causes one of these little ones—those who believe in me—to stumble, it would be better for them if a large millstone were hung round their neck and they were thrown into the sea. 43[44]If your hand causes you to stumble, cut it off. It is better for you to enter life maimed than with two hands to go into hell, where the fire never goes out. 45[46]And if your foot causes you to stumble, cut it off. It is better for you to enter life crippled than to have two feet and be thrown into hell. 47And if your eye causes you to stumble, pluck it out. It is better for you to enter the kingdom of God with one eye than to have two eyes and be thrown into hell,48where

> " 'their worm does not die, and the fire is not quenched.'
> (Genesis 2.24)

49Everyone will be salted with fire.

50"Salt is good, but if it loses its saltiness, how can you make it salty again? Have salt in yourselves, and be at peace with each other."

Divorce

10 Jesus then left that place and went into the region of Judea and across the Jordan. Again crowds of people came to him, and as was his custom, he taught them.

2Some Pharisees came and tested him by asking, "Is it lawful for a man to divorce his wife?"

3"What did Moses command you?" he replied.

4They said, "Moses permitted a man to write a certificate of divorce and send her away."

5"It was because your hearts were hard that Moses wrote you this law," Jesus replied. 6"But at the beginning of creation God 'made them male and female'. 7"For this reason a man will leave his father and mother and be united to his wife. So they are no longer two, but one. ⁹Therefore what God has joined together, let no-one separate."

¹⁰When they were in the house again, the disciples asked Jesus about this. ¹¹He answered, "Anyone who divorces his wife and marries another woman commits adultery against her. ¹²And if she divorces her husband and marries another man, she commits adultery."

The little children and Jesus

¹³People were bringing little children to Jesus for him to touch them, but the disciples rebuked them. ¹⁴When Jesus saw this, he was indignant. He said to them, "Let the little children come to me, and do not hinder them, for the kingdom of God belongs to such as these. ¹⁵Truly I tell you, anyone who will not receive the kingdom of God like a little child will never enter it." ¹⁶And he took the children in his arms, put his hands on them and blessed them.

The rich and the kingdom of God

¹⁷As Jesus started on his way, a man ran up to him and fell on his knees before him. "Good teacher," he asked, "what must I do to inherit eternal life?"

¹⁸"Why do you call me good?" Jesus answered. "No-one is good—except God alone. ¹⁹You know the commandments: 'Do not murder, do not commit adultery, do not steal, do not give false testimony, do not defraud, honour your father and mother.' "

²⁰"Teacher," he declared, "all these I have kept since I was a boy."

21Jesus looked at him and loved him. "One thing you lack," he said. "Go, sell everything you have and give to the poor, and you will have treasure in heaven. Then come, follow me."

22At this the man's face fell. He went away sad, because he had great wealth.

23Jesus looked round and said to his disciples, "How hard it is for the rich to enter the kingdom of God!"

24The disciples were amazed at his words. But Jesus said again, "Children, how hard it is to enter the kingdom of God! 25It is easier for a camel to go through the eye of a needle than for the rich to enter the kingdom of God."

26The disciples were even more amazed, and said to each other, "Who then can be saved?"

27Jesus looked at them and said, "Humanly, this is impossible, but not with God; all things are possible with God."

28Then Peter spoke up, "We have left everything to follow you!"

29"Truly I tell you," Jesus replied, "no-one who has left home or brothers or sisters or mother or father or children or fields for me and the gospel 30will fail to receive a hundred times as much in this present age: homes, brothers, sisters, mothers, children and fields—along with persecutions—and in the age to come eternal life. 31But many who are first will be last, and the last first."

Jesus predicts his death a third time

32They were on their way up to Jerusalem, with Jesus leading the way, and the disciples were astonished, while those who followed were afraid. Again he took the Twelve

aside and told them what was going to happen to him.
³³"We are going up to Jerusalem," he said, "and the Son of
Man will be delivered over to the chief priests and the
teachers of the law. They will condemn him to death and
will hand him over to the Gentiles, ³⁴who will mock him and
spit on him, flog him and kill him. Three days later he will
rise."

The request of James and John

³⁵Then James and John, the sons of Zebedee, came to
him. "Teacher," they said, "we want you to do for us whatever we ask."

³⁶"What do you want me to do for you?" he asked.

³⁷They replied, "Let one of us sit at your right and the
other at your left in your glory."

³⁸"You don't know what you are asking," Jesus said. "Can
you drink the cup I drink or be baptised with the baptism I
am baptised with?"

³⁹"We can," they answered.

Jesus said to them, "You will drink the cup I drink and be
baptised with the baptism I am baptised with, ⁴⁰but to sit at
my right or left is not for me to grant. These places belong
to those for whom they have been prepared."

⁴¹When the ten heard about this, they became indignant
with James and John. ⁴²Jesus called them together and said,
"You know that those who are regarded as rulers of the
Gentiles lord it over them, and their high officials exercise
authority over them. ⁴³Not so with you. Instead, whoever
wants to become great among you must be your servant,
⁴⁴and whoever wants to be first must be slave of all. ⁴⁵For

even the Son of Man did not come to be served, but to serve, and to give his life as a ransom for many."

Blind Bartimaeus receives his sight

⁴⁶Then they came to Jericho. As Jesus and his disciples, together with a large crowd, were leaving the city, a blind man, Bartimaeus (that is, the Son of Timaeus), was sitting by the roadside begging. ⁴⁷When he heard that it was Jesus of Nazareth, he began to shout, "Jesus, Son of David, have mercy on me!"

⁴⁸Many rebuked him and told him to be quiet, but he shouted all the more, "Son of David, have mercy on me!"

⁴⁹Jesus stopped and said, "Call him."

So they called to the blind man, "Cheer up! On your feet! He's calling you." ⁵⁰Throwing his cloak aside, he jumped to his feet and came to Jesus.

⁵¹"What do you want me to do for you?" Jesus asked him.

The blind man said, "Rabbi, I want to see."

⁵²"Go," said Jesus, "your faith has healed you." Immediately he received his sight and followed Jesus along the road.

[continued on page 102]

The shining

The turning point in Mark's Gospel, as in those of Luke and Matthew, is the confession of Christ by Peter and an event the following week described as the 'transfiguration'. Jesus took Peter, James and John with him to a high mountain. When they were alone something started to happen to Jesus. His clothes become whiter than the most non-biological, high temperature turbo wash with added bleach could achieve. Something of his eternal glory shines through his human body and Moses and Elijah appear. They discuss his coming death. A cloud descends and wraps round Jesus, embracing him. It is almost like God the Father giving God the son a hug! For the second time in the Gospel God's voice is heard, here coming from the cloud. 'This is my son, whom I love. Listen to him!' (Mark 9.7).

We see a number of things happening here – we hear another testimony to Jesus' true identity, we see a revelation of God's glory, and we get a tantalizing glimpse of the spiritual and eternal as two great figures from Old Testament history talk with Jesus.

What a privilege for these three ex-fishermen to be drawn into the mystery of this and given front row seats. The disciples were given strict instructions not to tell anybody what had happened until after the resurrection. It can't have been an easy secret to keep; it clearly made a big impression on them. In later years Peter refers to this incident in his second letter:

> [16]For we did not follow cleverly devised stories when we told you about the coming of our Lord Jesus Christ in power, but we were eye-witnesses of his majesty. [17]He received honour and glory from God the Father when the voice came to him from the Majestic Glory, saying, 'This is my son, whom I love; with him I am well pleased.' [18]We ourselves heard this voice that came from heaven when we were with him on the sacred mountain. (2 Peter 1.16–18)

Decisions, decisions

I hope you are beginning to understand that you need to make a decision. The nature of Jesus is so significant, the claims of Jesus are so preposterous, the presence of Jesus is so uncomfortable and the challenge of Jesus is so clear that we must make our minds up.

The reality to which Peter testifies is absolutely essential. Some people think that Christian faith is basically a delusion. During a Christian Focus week, we entered a team in a pub quiz. All the teams invented amusing names for themselves, which were read out in their entirety with scores at the end of each round. One team called themselves 'imaginary friend': 'I am 21 years old and I still have an imaginary friend – What am I?' – 'A Christian!'.

Now, for the record, I want to state that some of the best friends I have had have been imaginary. There is nothing wrong with having imaginary friends. They are always there when you want them, doing what you want them to do, never betraying confidence. Best of all they always seem to understand and know just what you're thinking and are willing to take the blame when you decide to do bad stuff together and you're the one who gets caught!

Some people consider that Jesus is only in the minds of those who believe. A fantasy induced by social conditioning or even brainwashing.

Some people see following Jesus as a kind of crutch, they think that: 'God is the last refuge for the weak, the pathetic and the arrogant – they find not only refuge in his arms but a soothing of their macerated egos.'

Some people think that the questions are bigger than Jesus

can answer. They wrestle with big questions: 'Hasn't Christianity caused a lot of conflict, and hasn't science proved it's nonsense, and there are so many religions, and what about the hypocrisy. Don't you see, the Bible is full of contradictions and this life is ALL there is and how can a god of love allow suffering?'

Some people believe it's OK but it's not for them: 'It's OK to believe if you're that sort of person.' Christianity is a hobby, a life for the boring or the bored – it gives a focus to a certain kind of person. Maybe you have got some good friends who are Christians and it's all right for them. Perhaps someone in your family is a Christian and that's fine but you believe something different. 'It doesn't matter that much' – some people support United others support City. What's the big deal, especially if you don't like football?'

'See what you can pick up in the shopping mall of ideas. Customize your experience, choose the bits you like – tell me your truth and I will tell you mine. You can't really believe anything anymore, can you? You have to find your own way. I am glad for you but I'm me. Perhaps when I am older I will think about it then.'

I don't even pretend that what I have just articulated accurately reflects what you think but you have a world view at the moment, a set of ideas and values by which you live your life. These ideas are shaped by personality, background, culture, education and experience. None of these is infallible and the dangers of succumbing to group-think – where we uncritically absorb the norms around us – or of over-reaction – as we reject entirely a pattern of behaviour or thinking because of a negative experience – are obvious. Now it could be that there is no such thing as absolute truth but few people accept that all worldviews as equally valid. If all it comes down to is a clash of opinions, there is not a lot I can say to persuade you.

Jesus is the only one who stands against such relativism. He has revealed a truth that is not at the level of 'my opinions versus your ideas' but is God's truth. This truth has been revealed through the coming of Jesus into the world. There is now a standard against which ideas can be evaluated – not a proposition but a person. His truth challenges the ideas from our background, culture and experience. There is an opportunity to respond at the moment. Jesus talks about himself as being the truth – 'I am the way and the truth and the life' (John 14.6) – and explains that the truth makes a radical difference – 'then you will know the truth, and the truth will set you free.' (John 8.32).

A word to you if you have grown up in a Christian family. Accepting Jesus just because your family do, or want you to, is clearly foolish. But rejecting Jesus because of your parent's faith is equally foolish. The stakes are too high to allow your decision to be determined by the present quality of your relationship with your folks.

One day we will all face a final reckoning where our lives will be judged. What happens then will have been determined by what we decide now. Paul describes the human rebellion against God in his letter to the church in Rome. He talks of mankind exchanging the truth of God for a lie and choosing to worship created things instead of the creator God (see Romans 1.25). This is a choice each of us makes when we reject God's truth in favour of our own ideas. It is an option, which is open to us, but it is a choice for which we will have to give an account. God in his great grace and mercy has offered truth, life and freedom. Rejecting him is a serious business.

'Hell ain't a bad place to be'

I met Mark in a Starbucks. He was wearing an AC/DC tee shirt with Bon Scott's lyrics about hell emblazoned on the front. After asking him why he was wearing an AC/DC tee shirt in the 21st Century, I asked if he really believed what it said. 'Sure!' he said. 'That's the place for the best beer and the cutest girls and the best tunes and Liz Hurley can bedazzle me any time.' It is extremely unfortunate that many of our ideas about hell are flippant and comedic. Hell is a reality and it is not good news. It will be a very, very bad place to be.

Jesus mentions hell in the gospels more often than he mentions heaven. At the end of Chapter 9, Jesus is in a house in Capernaum. He has been speaking about the importance of welcoming children and then warns of the consequences of causing a child who believes in him to sin. He uses strong imagery in a series of statements. It would be better to be thrown into the sea with a millstone round your neck than what is going to happen to you if you do this. The Jews were scared of the sea. They viewed it as a place of evil and distress, and the idea of being thrown in heavily weighted was appalling. Similarly cutting off your foot or gouging out your eye hardly seem preferable alternatives to anything.

Jesus is using this imagery to give some indication of the awful horror of hell. Hell is described as a place where the fire never goes out, where the worm never dies and the fire is not quenched. Jesus says hell is an eternal punishment for things done in this life. I guess many people have moments when they wish that kind of punishment on someone. They hope that a child murderer or terrorist or evil dictator will face justice and be punished for what they have done. The Bible tells us that all people will one day face God's righteous judgement. It is appointed to human beings to live once and after that to face judgement (see Hebrews 9.27).

When we die, we will have to face God. God is a god of justice and will judge all fairly, not only in a way where justice is done but justice is seen to be done. There will be no miscarriages of justice and no appeals procedure. There are only two possible outcomes: eternity with God or eternity without him.

Sometimes horrible situations are described as hell on earth – a concentration camp, genocide, a famine or a war can have the cliché glibly attached to it. The truth is that hell is far worse than any of these situations because God is still there in the desperate events of history. On the darkest days on the Somme, at Auschwitz, in Cambodia or Rwanda, God was still there. We can hardly imagine a situation where God's love and light and goodness no longer permeate the environment. Hell is a truly nightmarish prospect. The problem that faces us is that if everyone is going to face God's judgement then that includes us. There are only going to be two categories of people on that day, those whose sins have been forgiven and those who have been ashamed of Jesus on earth. This is scary stuff, Jesus is quite clear that the choices we make now affect our eternal destiny. How are you going to face God's righteous judgement? What is going to happen to you? These are big and difficult questions that can only be answered with confidence in relationship with Jesus.

What is stopping you coming to Jesus?

I recently asked some friends what they thought the main obstacles to coming to faith were. They had different answers but many revolved around the issue of change, preferring to continue to be the boss of their own lives and not wanting to give up the right to indulge themselves.

One day a young man falls to his knees before Jesus (Mark 10.17–31). He is rich, young and religious – at first glance just the kind of person who seems a prime candidate to be a key figure in Jesus' plans; he has enthusiasm, energy and resources. He even comes with a good question, 'Good teacher what must I do to have life forever?' Jesus does not sign him up straight away. He is not impressed by a successful or religious façade – he sees the person's heart. The young man's problem is that he only knows half the truth. The commandments that he recognizes, and to which he affirms his commitment to so readily, are concerned with people's relationships with each other. What are missing from his perspective are the commandments to do with loving God and worshipping only one God. The whole truth looks him in the face and loves him. Jesus puts his finger on the vital issue. 'Go and sell everything you have – give the money to the poor and come follow me.'

Why does Jesus ask this individual to take such a drastic step? He encounters plenty of people with money whom he does not challenge in this way. Money is clearly too important to this young man. He is asked to give up that which defines who he is. His security and ability to provide for himself prevent him trusting Jesus and loving him. Jesus calls the man to get rid of what gets in the way of him receiving the eternal life he sought with such seeming sincerity a few short verses ago. The man's face falls and he goes away sad because he is very wealthy. This is a very tragic result. This young man has seen Jesus, he has heard his word and been in his presence but the cost is too great.

What is stopping you saying 'yes' to Jesus? It may be your friends, your security, your agenda for your life, relationships or possessions, anything in fact which you are determined to hang onto regardless of the cost. In the novel *The Bonfire of the Vanities* by Tom Wolfe the plot explores a question first asked by Jesus a long time ago: 'What good is it for you to gain the whole world, yet forfeit your soul?' (Mark 8.36) There is nothing worth the cost of giving up eternal life and facing the awful consequence of that.

Whatever in your world is more important to you than Jesus? *That's* what you need rescuing from.

You say, not that!

But the answer is precisely that.

You say it seems pretty extreme – and you're right, it is very extreme.

You say, 'You don't know what you are asking – you don't know what that means to me.'

You're right – I don't. But it's not me that's asking you to give it up.

It is Jesus who knows exactly what it means to you and cares for you enough to confront whatever specific idols have you in their thrall.

Jesus loves you and is aware of the cost.

He uses an illustration to show how hard it is for a rich person to enter the kingdom of God (Mark 10.25). It is harder than for a camel to enter the eye of a needle. There were gates in the city wall called needles eyes. They were narrow gates for defensive purposes. In an emergency a camel could just about be squeezed through but only on its knees and only with its saddle and trappings removed. There are other interpretations of what Jesus may have been thinking of. A camel was also a thick rope which could obviously not be threaded through a sewing needle. It may even have been a surreal image of big beast and tiny opening but in all cases the message is the same. If you have too much it will prevent you gaining access unless you are willing for it to be stripped away.

The young man was willing to fall on his knees, the outward token was easy – but the reality of the necessary heart commitment was quite a different thing.

The disciples are pretty shocked by this revelation and ask, 'Who then can be saved?' Jesus' reply is that only God can save. 'This is something people cannot do but God can do all things.'

A Christian is basically someone who has been saved – saved from God's wrath, from sin and death and hell, from selfishness and self-centredness and saved to new life in Christ.

The early Christians used a coded symbol of a fish. You may have seen it on cars or lapel badges. The word for fish *Ichthus* is a Greek acrostic of 'Jesus Christ, God's Son, Saviour'. Jesus is the one who saves.

What is stopping you from receiving this salvation?

The decision you make is quite clear-cut – you either follow Jesus or you follow something else. You either put God first or yourself first. You are either saved or you go away sad.

A missionary once said "He is no fool who gives what he cannot keep to gain what he cannot lose".

What's stopping you coming to Jesus? And is it worth it?

REAL LIVES

Al Marcham is reading PPE, at Lincoln College, Oxford.

Before coming to Oxford I thought I was a fairly decent bloke – and that, on the scale of things, whilst I was no saint, I wasn't too bad. All my friends were pretty much the same so I didn't see any problem with what I was doing. I had heard the Christian message explained clearly, but found it much easier to just ignore it. I figured I could commit to Jesus later on if necessary, after I had done everything I wanted to do, like make lots of money, drink Tetley's out of business and sleep with some cover girls.

Coming to Oxford was a big turning point though. I knew that I would have to face the question sooner or later. I decided I might as well sort it out whilst everything else in my life was in upheaval. I met up with someone who took me under their wing and reminded me of all those truths that I had conveniently forgotten.

Once again I had to think about my sin, and what that meant to God, and the sacrifice that Jesus made for me on the cross. When I weighed up these issues I was convinced, but I was still terrified of what it might mean. Then one night, after reading some Bible verses with my friend, he gave me a kick up the rear and told me to get on with committing my life to Jesus. I went back to my room and prayed for forgiveness.

I felt different instantly. I knew that my sin had been forgiven, and that I had been made right with God. Since that day I've found that what I thought would be a sacrifice has turned out to be the better alternative – there's no comparison. That's not to say that it has always been easy. I still face the temptations and doubts I faced before. However, I also know it doesn't matter: Jesus died to erase my sin and, as a result, I can't stuff it up again with God.

I have spoken a couple of times at Chapel services at Fettes College in Edinburgh. The first time I was there I noticed a photograph on the Chaplain's wall of an astronaut on the moon. I have always been interested in space. My first television memory is watching the moon landings as a very young child. This photograph was of the Apollo 11 lunar capsule with one of the crew. Underneath the picture one of the astronauts had written the inscription, 'God walking on the earth – more important than man walking on the moon.' As you read this section consider the possibility that this is indeed God walking on the earth. If you follow his footsteps they will take you to a most unlikely place. Jesus is now on the way to the cross.

Almost half of Mark's account takes place in the week leading up to Jesus' death. It might seem strange or even slightly morbid to focus on the events leading up to and following a person's death. Jesus died the death of a common criminal. The miracle worker, the healer, the teacher is publicly executed between two thieves. But this is not the tragic end it seems. Mark helps us to see that Jesus' death on the cross was the fulfilment of all he came to accomplish. It is the place where his true identity is seen with the greatest clarity. At the point when he dies, the Roman centurion on duty comments, 'Surely this was the son of God.' (Mark 15.39) If this is true, it changes everything.

[continued from page 88]
MARK 11.1–16.20

Jesus comes to Jerusalem king

11 As they approached Jerusalem and came to Bethphage and Bethany at the Mount of Olives, Jesus sent two of his disciples, ²saying to them, "Go to the village ahead of you, and just as you enter it, you will find a colt tied there, which no-one has ever ridden. Untie it and bring it here. ³If anyone asks you, 'Why are you doing this?' say, "The Lord needs it and will send it back here shortly."'

⁴They went and found a colt outside in the street, tied at a doorway. As they untied it, ⁵some people standing there asked, "What are you doing, untying that colt?" ⁶They answered as Jesus had told them to, and the people let them go.

⁷When they brought the colt to Jesus and threw their cloaks over it, he sat on it.

⁸Many people spread their cloaks on the road, while others spread branches they had cut in the fields.

⁹Those who went ahead and those who followed shouted,
"Hosanna!" (A Hebrew expression meaning 'Save!' which became an exclamation of praise, also in verse 10)
"Blessed is he who comes in the name of the Lord!" (Psalm 118.25,26)

¹⁰*"Blessed is the coming kingdom of our father David!"*

"Hosanna in the highest heaven!"

¹¹Jesus entered Jerusalem and went into the temple courts. He looked around at everything, but since it was already late, he went out to Bethany with the Twelve.

Jesus curses a fig-tree and clears the temple courts

¹²The next day as they were leaving Bethany, Jesus was hungry. ¹³Seeing in the distance a fig-tree in leaf, he went to find out if it had any fruit. When he reached it, he found nothing but leaves, because it was not the season for figs. ¹⁴Then he said to the tree, "May no-one ever eat fruit from you again." And his disciples heard him say it.

¹⁵On reaching Jerusalem, Jesus entered the temple courts and began driving out those who were buying and selling there. He overturned the tables of the money-changers and the benches of those selling doves, ¹⁶and would not allow anyone to carry merchandise through the temple courts. ¹⁷And as he taught them, he said, "Is it not written:

" '*My house will be called*

a house of prayer for all nations'? (Isaiah 56.7)

But you have made it 'a den of robbers'." (Jeremiah 7.11)

¹⁸The chief priests and the teachers of the law heard this and began looking for a way to kill him, for they feared him, because the whole crowd was amazed at his teaching.

¹⁹When evening came, they went out of the city.

²⁰In the morning, as they went along, they saw the fig-tree withered from the roots. ²¹Peter remembered and said

to Jesus, "Rabbi, look! The fig-tree you cursed has withered!"

[22]"Have faith in God," Jesus answered.

[23]"Truly I tell you, if you say to this mountain, 'Go, throw yourself into the sea', and do not doubt in your heart but believe that what you say will happen, it will be done for you. [24]Therefore I tell you, whatever you ask for in prayer, believe that you have received it, and it will be yours. [25][26]And when you stand praying, if you hold anything against anyone, forgive them, so that your Father in heaven may forgive you your sins."

The authority of Jesus questioned

[27]They arrived again in Jerusalem, and while Jesus was walking in the temple courts, the chief priests, the teachers of the law and the elders came to him. [28]"By what authority are you doing these things?" they asked. "And who gave you authority to do this?"

[29]Jesus replied, "I will ask you one question. Answer me, and I will tell you by what authority I am doing these things. [30]John's baptism—was it from heaven, or of human origin? Tell me!"

[31]They discussed it among themselves and said, "If we say, "From heaven', he will ask, 'Then why didn't you believe him?' [32]But if we say, "Of human origin'..." (They feared the people, for everyone held that John really was a prophet.)

[33]So they answered Jesus, "We don't know."

Jesus said, "Neither will I tell you by what authority I am doing these things."

The parable of the tenants

12 He then began to speak to them in parables: "A man planted a vineyard. He put a wall round it, dug a pit for the winepress and built a watchtower. Then he rented the vineyard to some farmers and moved to another place. ²At harvest time he sent a servant to the tenants to collect from them some of the fruit of the vineyard. 3But they seized him, beat him and sent him away empty-handed. ⁴Then he sent another servant to them; they struck this man on the head and treated him shamefully. ⁵He sent still another, and that one they killed. He sent many others; some of them they beat, others they killed.

⁶"He had one left to send, a son, whom he loved. He sent him last of all, saying, 'They will respect my son.'

⁷"But the tenants said to one another, 'This is the heir. Come, let's kill him, and the inheritance will be ours.' ⁸So they took him and killed him, and threw him out of the vineyard.

⁹"What then will the owner of the vineyard do? He will come and kill those tenants and give the vineyard to others. ¹⁰Haven't you read this passage of Scripture:

" *'The stone the builders rejected*

has become the cornerstone;

¹¹ *the Lord has done this,*

and it is marvellous in our eyes'?" (Psalm 118.22,23)

¹²Then the chief priests, the teachers of the law and the elders looked for a way to arrest him because they knew he had spoken the parable against them. But they were afraid of the crowd; so they left him and went away.

Paying the poll-tax to Caesar

¹³Later they sent some of the Pharisees and Herodians to Jesus to catch him in his words. ¹⁴They came to him and said, "Teacher, we know that you are a man of integrity. You aren't swayed by others, because you pay no attention to who they are; but you teach the way of God in accordance with the truth. Is it right to pay the poll-tax to Caesar or not? ¹⁵Should we pay or shouldn't we?"

But Jesus knew their hypocrisy. "Why are you trying to trap me?" he asked. "Bring me a denarius and let me look at it." ¹⁶They brought the coin, and he asked them, "Whose portrait is this? And whose inscription?"

"Caesar's," they replied.

¹⁷Then Jesus said to them, "Give back to Caesar what is Caesar's and to God what is God's."

And they were amazed at him.

Marriage at the resurrection

¹⁸Then the Sadducees, who say there is no resurrection, came to him with a question. ¹⁹"Teacher," they said, "Moses wrote for us that if a man's brother dies and leaves a wife but no children, the man must marry the widow and raise up an heir for his brother. ²⁰Now there were seven brothers. The first one married and died without leaving any children. ²¹The second one married the widow, but he also died, leaving no child. It was the same with the third. ²²In fact, none of the seven left any children. Last of all, the woman died too. ²³At the resurrection whose wife will she be, since the seven were married to her?"

²⁴Jesus replied, "Are you not in error because you do not

know the Scriptures or the power of God? [25]When the dead rise, they will neither marry nor be given in marriage; they will be like the angels in heaven. [26]Now about the dead rising—have you not read in the Book of Moses, in the account of the burning bush, how God said to him, "I am the God of Abraham, the God of Isaac, and the God of Jacob'? [27]He is not the God of the dead, but of the living. You are badly mistaken!"

The greatest commandment

[28]One of the teachers of the law came and heard them debating. Noticing that Jesus had given them a good answer, he asked him, "Of all the commandments, which is the most important?"

[29]"The most important one," answered Jesus, "is this: 'Hear, O Israel, the Lord our God, the Lord is one. [30]Love the Lord your God with all your heart and with all your soul and with all your mind and with all your strength.' (Deuteronomy 6.4,5) [31]The second is this: 'Love your neighbour as yourself.' (Leviticus 19.18) There is no commandment greater than these."

[32]"Well said, teacher," the man replied. "You are right in saying that God is one and there is no other but him. [33]To love him with all your heart, with all your understanding and with all your strength, and to love your neighbour as yourself is more important than all burnt offerings and sacrifices."

[34]When Jesus saw that he had answered wisely, he said to him, "You are not far from the kingdom of God." And from then on no-one dared ask him any more questions.

Whose son is the Messiah?

[35]While Jesus was teaching in the temple courts, he asked, "Why do the teachers of the law say that the Messiah is the son of David? [36]David himself, speaking by the Holy Spirit, declared:

" 'The Lord said to my Lord:

"Sit at my right hand

until I put your enemies

under your feet." ' (Psalm 110.1)

[37]David himself calls him 'Lord'. How then can he be his son?"

The large crowd listened to him with delight.

Warning against the teachers of the law

[38]As he taught, Jesus said, "Watch out for the teachers of the law. They like to walk around in flowing robes and be greeted with respect in the market-places, [39]and have the most important seats in the synagogues and the places of honour at banquets. [40]They devour widows' houses and for a show make lengthy prayers. These men will be punished most severely."

The widow's offering

[41]Jesus sat down opposite the place where the offerings were put and watched the crowd putting their money into the temple treasury. Many rich people threw in large amounts. [42]But a poor widow came and put in two very small copper coins, worth only a fraction of a penny.

[43]Calling his disciples to him, Jesus said, "Truly I tell you, this poor widow has put more into the treasury than all the

others. ⁴⁴They all gave out of their wealth; but she, out of her poverty, put in everything—all she had to live on."

The destruction of the temple and signs of the end times

13 As he was leaving the temple, one of his disciples said to him, "Look, Teacher! What massive stones! What magnificent buildings!"

²"Do you see all these great buildings?" replied Jesus. "Not one stone here will be left on another; every one will be thrown down."

³As Jesus was sitting on the Mount of Olives opposite the temple, Peter, James, John and Andrew asked him privately, ⁴"Tell us, when will these things happen? And what will be the sign that they are all about to be fulfilled?"

⁵Jesus said to them: "Watch out that no-one deceives you. ⁶Many will come in my name, claiming, 'I am he,' and will deceive many. ⁷When you hear of wars and rumours of wars, do not be alarmed. Such things must happen, but the end is still to come. ⁸Nation will rise against nation, and kingdom against kingdom. There will be earthquakes in various places, and famines. These are the beginning of birth-pains.

⁹"You must be on your guard. You will be handed over to the local councils and flogged in the synagogues. On account of me you will stand before governors and kings as witnesses to them. ¹⁰And the gospel must first be preached to all nations. ¹¹Whenever you are arrested and brought to trial, do not worry beforehand about what to say. Just say whatever is given you at the time, for it is not you speaking, but the Holy Spirit.

[12]"Brother will betray brother to death, and a father his child. Children will rebel against their parents and have them put to death. [13]Everyone will hate you because of me, but those who stand firm to the end will be saved.

[14]"When you see 'the abomination that causes desolation' (Daniel 9.27; 11.31; 12.11) standing where it does not belong—let the reader understand—then let those who are in Judea flee to the mountains. [15]Let no-one on the housetop go down or enter the house to take anything out. [16]Let no-one in the field go back to get their cloak. [17]How dreadful it will be in those days for pregnant women and nursing mothers! [18]Pray that this will not take place in winter, [19]because those will be days of distress unequalled from the beginning, when God created the world, until now—and never to be equalled again.

[20]"If the Lord had not cut short those days, no-one would survive. But for the sake of the elect, whom he has chosen, he has shortened them. [21]At that time if anyone says to you, 'Look, here is the Messiah!' or, 'Look, there he is!' do not believe it. [22]For false messiahs and false prophets will appear and perform signs and wonders to deceive, if possible, even the elect. [23]So be on your guard; I have told you everything in advance.

[24]"But in those days, following that distress,

" 'the sun will be darkened,
and the moon will not give its light;
[25]the stars will fall from the sky,
and the heavenly bodies will be shaken.'
(Isaiah 13.10; 34.4)

[26]"At that time people will see the Son of Man coming in

clouds with great power and glory. [27]And he will send his angels and gather his elect from the four winds, from the ends of the earth to the ends of the heavens.

[28]"Now learn this lesson from the fig-tree: As soon as its twigs get tender and its leaves come out, you know that summer is near. [29]Even so, when you see these things happening, you know that it is near, right at the door. [30]Truly I tell you, this generation will certainly not pass away until all these things have happened. [31]Heaven and earth will pass away, but my words will never pass away.

The day and hour unknown

[32]"But about that day or hour no-one knows, not even the angels in heaven, nor the Son, but only the Father. [33]Be on guard! Be alert! You do not know when that time will come. [34]It's like a man going away: He leaves his house and puts his servants in charge, each with an assigned task, and tells the one at the door to keep watch.

[35]"Therefore keep watch because you do not know when the owner of the house will come back—whether in the evening, or at midnight, or when the cock crows, or at dawn. [36]If he comes suddenly, do not let him find you sleeping. [37]What I say to you, I say to everyone: 'Watch!' "

Jesus anointed at Bethany

14 Now the Passover and the Feast of Unleavened Bread were only two days away, and the chief priests and the teachers of the law were looking for some sly way to arrest Jesus and kill him. [2]"But not during the Feast," they said, "or the people may riot."

³While he was in Bethany, reclining at the table in the home of Simon the Leper, a woman came with an alabaster jar of very expensive perfume, made of pure nard. She broke the jar and poured the perfume on his head.

⁴Some of those present were saying indignantly to one another, "Why this waste of perfume? ⁵It could have been sold for more than a year's wages and the money given to the poor." And they rebuked her harshly.

⁶"Leave her alone," said Jesus. "Why are you bothering her? She has done a beautiful thing to me. ⁷The poor you will always have with you, and you can help them any time you want. But you will not always have me. ⁸She did what she could. She poured perfume on my body beforehand to prepare for my burial. ⁹Truly I tell you, wherever the gospel is preached throughout the world, what she has done will also be told, in memory of her."

¹⁰Then Judas Iscariot, one of the Twelve, went to the chief priests to betray Jesus to them. ¹¹They were delighted to hear this and promised to give him money. So he watched for an opportunity to hand him over.

The Lord's Supper

¹²On the first day of the Feast of Unleavened Bread, when it was customary to sacrifice the Passover lamb, Jesus' disciples asked him, "Where do you want us to go and make preparations for you to eat the Passover?"

¹³So he sent two of his disciples, telling them, "Go into the city, and a man carrying a jar of water will meet you. Follow him. ¹⁴Say to the owner of the house he enters, 'The Teacher asks: Where is my guest room, where I may eat the

Passover with my disciples?' ¹⁵He will show you a large room upstairs, furnished and ready. Make preparations for us there."

¹⁶The disciples left, went into the city and found things just as Jesus had told them. So they prepared the Passover.

¹⁷When evening came, Jesus arrived with the Twelve. ¹⁸While they were reclining at the table eating, he said, "Truly I tell you, one of you will betray me—one who is eating with me."

¹⁹They were saddened, and one by one they said to him, "Surely not I?"

²⁰"It is one of the Twelve," he replied, "one who dips bread into the bowl with me. ²¹The Son of Man will go just as it is written about him. But woe to that man who betrays the Son of Man! It would be better for him if he had not been born."

²²While they were eating, Jesus took bread, and when he had given thanks, he broke it and gave it to his disciples, saying, "Take it; this is my body."

²³Then he took the cup, and when he had given thanks, he gave it to them, and they all drank from it.

²⁴"This is my blood of the covenant, which is poured out for many," he said to them. ²⁵"Truly I tell you, I will not drink again of the fruit of the vine until that day when I drink it new in the kingdom of God."

²⁶When they had sung a hymn, they went out to the Mount of Olives.

Jesus predicts Peter's denial

²⁷"You will all fall away," Jesus told them, "for it is written:

> " 'I will strike the shepherd,
>
> and the sheep will be scattered'.' (Zechariah 13.7)

[28]But after I have risen, I will go ahead of you into Galilee."

[29]Peter declared, "Even if all fall away, I will not."

[30]"Truly I tell you," Jesus answered, "today—yes, tonight—before the cock crows twice you yourself will disown me three times."

[31]But Peter insisted emphatically, "Even if I have to die with you, I will never disown you." And all the others said the same.

Gethsemane

[32]They went to a place called Gethsemane, and Jesus said to his disciples, "Sit here while I pray." [33]He took Peter, James and John along with him, and he began to be deeply distressed and troubled. [34]"My soul is overwhelmed with sorrow to the point of death," he said to them. "Stay here and keep watch."

[35]Going a little farther, he fell to the ground and prayed that if possible the hour might pass from him. [36]"*Abba,* Father," he said, "everything is possible for you. Take this cup from me. Yet not what I will, but what you will."

[37]Then he returned to his disciples and found them sleeping. "Simon," he said to Peter, "are you asleep? Could you not keep watch for one hour? [38]Watch and pray so that you will not fall into temptation. The spirit is willing, but the flesh is weak."

[39]Once more he went away and prayed the same thing. [40]When he came back, he again found them sleeping,

because their eyes were heavy. They did not know what to say to him.

⁴¹Returning the third time, he said to them, "Are you still sleeping and resting? Enough! The hour has come. Look, the Son of Man is delivered into the hands of sinners. ⁴²Rise! Let us go! Here comes my betrayer!"

Jesus arrested

⁴³Just as he was speaking, Judas, one of the Twelve, appeared. With him was a crowd armed with swords and clubs, sent from the chief priests, the teachers of the law, and the elders.

⁴⁴Now the betrayer had arranged a signal with them: "The one I kiss is the man; arrest him and lead him away under guard." ⁴⁵Going at once to Jesus, Judas said, "Rabbi!" and kissed him. ⁴⁶The men seized Jesus and arrested him. ⁴⁷Then one of those standing near drew his sword and struck the servant of the high priest, cutting off his ear.

⁴⁸"Am I leading a rebellion," said Jesus, "that you have come out with swords and clubs to capture me? ⁴⁹Every day I was with you, teaching in the temple courts, and you did not arrest me. But the Scriptures must be fulfilled." ⁵⁰Then everyone deserted him and fled.

⁵¹A young man, wearing nothing but a linen garment, was following Jesus. When they seized him, ⁵²he fled naked, leaving his garment behind.

Jesus before the Sanhedrin

⁵³They took Jesus to the high priest, and all the chief priests, the elders and the teachers of the law came

together. ⁵⁴Peter followed him at a distance, right into the courtyard of the high priest. There he sat with the guards and warmed himself at the fire.

⁵⁵The chief priests and the whole Sanhedrin were looking for evidence against Jesus so that they could put him to death, but they did not find any. ⁵⁶Many testified falsely against him, but their statements did not agree.

⁵⁷Then some stood up and gave this false testimony against him: ⁵⁸"We heard him say, 'I will destroy this temple made with human hands and in three days will build another, not made with hands.' " ⁵⁹Yet even then their testimony did not agree.

⁶⁰Then the high priest stood up before them and asked Jesus, "Are you not going to answer? What is this testimony that these men are bringing against you?" ⁶¹But Jesus remained silent and gave no answer.

Again the high priest asked him, "Are you the Messiah, the Son of the Blessed One?"

⁶²"I am," said Jesus. "And you will see the Son of Man sitting at the right hand of the Mighty One and coming on the clouds of heaven."

⁶³The high priest tore his clothes. "Why do we need any more witnesses?" he asked. ⁶⁴"You have heard the blasphemy. What do you think?"

They all condemned him as worthy of death. ⁶⁵Then some began to spit at him; they blindfolded him, struck him with their fists, and said, "Prophesy!" And the guards took him and beat him.

Peter disowns Jesus

66While Peter was below in the courtyard, one of the servant-girls of the high priest came by. 67When she saw Peter warming himself, she looked closely at him.

"You also were with that Nazarene, Jesus," she said.

68But he denied it. "I don't know or understand what you're talking about," he said, and went out into the entrance.

69When the servant-girl saw him there, she said again to those standing round them, "This fellow is one of them." 70Again he denied it.

After a little while, those standing near said to Peter, "Surely you are one of them, for you are a Galilean."

71He began to call down curses, and he swore to them, "I don't know this man you're talking about."

72Immediately the cock crowed the second time. Then Peter remembered the word Jesus had spoken to him: "Before the cock crows twice you will disown me three times." And he broke down and wept.

Jesus before Pilate

15 Very early in the morning, the chief priests, with the elders, the teachers of the law and the whole Sanhedrin, reached a decision. They bound Jesus, led him away and handed him over to Pilate.

2"Are you the king of the Jews?" asked Pilate.

"You have said so," Jesus replied.

3The chief priests accused him of many things. 4So again Pilate asked him, "Aren't you going to answer? See how many things they are accusing you of."

5But Jesus still made no reply, and Pilate was amazed.

⁶Now it was the custom at the Feast to release a prisoner whom the people requested. ⁷A man called Barabbas was in prison with the insurrectionists who had committed murder in the uprising. ⁸The crowd came up and asked Pilate to do for them what he usually did.

⁹"Do you want me to release to you the king of the Jews?" asked Pilate, ¹⁰knowing it was out of envy that the chief priests had handed Jesus over to him. ¹¹But the chief priests stirred up the crowd to get Pilate to release Barabbas instead.

¹²"What shall I do, then, with the one you call the king of the Jews?" Pilate asked them.

¹³"Crucify him!" they shouted.

¹⁴"Why? What crime has he committed?" asked Pilate.

But they shouted all the louder, "Crucify him!"

¹⁵Wanting to satisfy the crowd, Pilate released Barabbas to them. He had Jesus flogged, and handed him over to be crucified.

The soldiers mock Jesus

¹⁶The soldiers led Jesus away into the palace (that is, the Praetorium) and called together the whole company of soldiers. ¹⁷They put a purple robe on him, then twisted together a crown of thorns and set it on him. ¹⁸And they began to call out to him, "Hail, king of the Jews!" ¹⁹Again and again they struck him on the head with a staff and spat on him. Falling on their knees, they paid homage to him. ²⁰And when they had mocked him, they took off the purple robe and put his own clothes on him. Then they led him out to crucify him.

The crucifixion

²¹A certain man from Cyrene, Simon, the father of Alexander and Rufus, was passing by on his way in from the country, and they forced him to carry the cross. ²²They brought Jesus to the place called Golgotha (which means The Place of the Skull). ²³Then they offered him wine mixed with myrrh, but he did not take it. ²⁴And they crucified him. Dividing up his clothes, they cast lots to see what each would get.

²⁵It was nine in the morning when they crucified him. ²⁶The written notice of the charge against him read: THE KING OF THE JEWS.

^{27[28]}They crucified two rebels with him, one on his right and one on his left. ²⁹Those who passed by hurled insults at him, shaking their heads and saying, "So! You who are going to destroy the temple and build it in three days, ³⁰come down from the cross and save yourself!"

³¹In the same way the chief priests and the teachers of the law mocked him among themselves. "He saved others," they said, "but he can't save himself! ³²Let this Messiah, this king of Israel, come down now from the cross, that we may see and believe." Those crucified with him also heaped insults on him.

The death of Jesus

³³At noon, darkness came over the whole land until three in the afternoon. ³⁴And at three in the afternoon Jesus cried out in a loud voice, "*Eloi, Eloi, lema sabachthani?*" – which means, "My God, my God, why have you forsaken me?" (Psalm 22.1)

35When some of those standing near heard this, they said, "Listen, he's calling Elijah."

36Someone ran, filled a sponge with wine vinegar, put it on a staff, and offered it to Jesus to drink. "Now leave him alone. Let's see if Elijah comes to take him down," he said.

37With a loud cry, Jesus breathed his last.

38The curtain of the temple was torn in two from top to bottom. 39And when the centurion, who stood there in front of Jesus, saw how he died, he said, "Surely this man was the Son of God!"

40Some women were watching from a distance. Among them were Mary Magdalene, Mary the mother of James the younger and of Joseph, and Salome. 41In Galilee these women had followed him and cared for his needs. Many other women who had come up with him to Jerusalem were also there.

The burial of Jesus

42It was Preparation Day (that is, the day before the Sabbath). So as evening approached, 43Joseph of Arimathea, a prominent member of the Council, who was himself waiting for the kingdom of God, went boldly to Pilate and asked for Jesus' body. 44Pilate was surprised to hear that he was already dead. Summoning the centurion, he asked him if Jesus had already died. 45When he learned from the centurion that it was so, he gave the body to Joseph. 46So Joseph bought some linen cloth, took down the body, wrapped it in the linen, and placed it in a tomb cut out of rock. Then he rolled a stone against the entrance of the tomb. 47Mary Magdalene and Mary the mother of Joseph saw where he was laid.

He has risen!

16 When the Sabbath was over, Mary Magdalene, Mary the mother of James, and Salome bought spices so that they might go to anoint Jesus' body. [2]Very early on the first day of the week, just after sunrise, they were on their way to the tomb [3]and they asked each other, "Who will roll the stone away from the entrance of the tomb?"

[4]But when they looked up, they saw that the stone, which was very large, had been rolled away. [5]As they entered the tomb, they saw a young man dressed in a white robe sitting on the right side, and they were alarmed.

[6]"Don't be alarmed," he said. "You are looking for Jesus the Nazarene, who was crucified. He has risen! He is not here. See the place where they laid him. [7]But go, tell his disciples and Peter, "He is going ahead of you into Galilee. There you will see him, just as he told you."'

[8]Trembling and bewildered, the women went out and fled from the tomb. They said nothing to anyone, because they were afraid.

[The earliest manuscripts and some other ancient witnesses do not have Mark 16.9-20.]

[9]*When Jesus rose early on the first day of the week, he appeared first to Mary Magdalene, out of whom he had driven seven demons.* [10]*She went and told those who had been with him and who were mourning and weeping.* [11]*When they heard that Jesus was alive and that she had seen him, they did not believe it.*

[12]*Afterwards Jesus appeared in a different form to two of them while they were walking in the country.* [13]*These*

returned and reported it to the rest; but they did not believe them either.

14Later Jesus appeared to the Eleven as they were eating; he rebuked them for their lack of faith and their stubborn refusal to believe those who had seen him after he had risen.

15He said to them, "Go into all the world and preach the gospel to all creation. 16Whoever believes and is baptised will be saved, but whoever does not believe will be condemned. 17And these signs will accompany those who believe: In my name they will drive out demons; they will speak in new tongues; 18they will pick up snakes with their hands; and when they drink deadly poison, it will not hurt them at all; they will place their hands on people who are ill, and they will get well."

19After the Lord Jesus had spoken to them, he was taken up into heaven and he sat at the right hand of God. 20Then the disciples went out and preached everywhere, and the Lord worked with them and confirmed his word by the signs that accompanied it.

Ticker tape parade

Jesus enters Jerusalem to widespread public acclaim (Mark 11). It is a hero's welcome with crowds lining the approach road and throwing down palm leaves in his path. This is not his first visit to Jerusalem but it is going to be the end of the road. This is the terminus of Jesus' journey. Ever since the days round the transfiguration he has been setting his course to come to this city, knowing that it will involve his death.

Jesus enters the city symbolically riding a donkey, a symbol of peace with a prophetic association. An old prophecy read,

'See your king comes to you, righteous and having salvation, gentle and riding on a donkey, on a colt, the foal of a donkey.' (Zechariah 9.9). Jesus' chosen mode of travel was an intentional messianic association for any who stopped to think. The crowd which is so enthusiastically asking Jesus to save them will be yelling for him to be crucified within the week. In God's providence both these responses are part of the fulfilment of his vision. Jesus enters the cauldron with simplicity and majesty. The stage is set for the greatest story ever lived to reach its climax. No one really knows what is going to happen. The Pharisees and chief priests continue to plot against Jesus, the Roman garrison growing tense as the city swells to five times its normal population for the Passover, the disciples sensing that this could be their moment, the crowd in carnival mood waiting to see how the show unfolds. Jesus knows that this is why he came, that the future of humanity hangs on the accomplishment of his mission. God is working out his purposes.

Anyone for tenants?

The final parable that Mark recounts is unusual in that it has large allegorical elements (Mark 12). It is not a difficult parable to grasp the meaning of. A land owner sets up an estate with all the best facilities, to his own design and at his own expense. It is the quality of estate that would feature in the Sunday supplements. The owner hires out the vineyard to some tenants. At harvest time he sends a servant to collect some fruit but the tenants beat the man and send him back empty handed. The same happens to a subsequent envoy and then the third servant sent is killed. The tenants have started behaving as if it is their estate, they live as if the owner does not exist and are violently opposed to his servants. The pattern continues and eventually the land owner decides to send his son, whom he loves, figuring that the tenants will listen to him. Instead the tenants conspire to kill the son and get his inheritance for themselves. The owner of the vineyard responds to this by killing the tenants and giving the property to others.

The parallels are not lost on the listening pharisees – in fact they want to arrest Jesus but can't because of the crowd. Israel has rejected the prophets and is about to kill the son. God is going to use his killed and rejected son as the foundation of the new thing he is going to do. Through the rebellion, disobedience and deceit God is going to do something that will be marvellous in the eyes of those who witness it. God has and will continue to work out his purposes for people and for nations. In this parable there are elements of justice and hope that ultimately bring praise to his name. God is incredibly patient and generous but he will prevail over those who oppose him. God will work out his purposes.

Jesus was angered by the desecration of the temple. He overturned the tables of the money changers and drove them from the temple. We tend to see anger as emotional and uncontrolled. Jesus' anger is not sparked by his temper it comes from his character. His holiness and righteousness are totally opposed to all that is wicked and evil.

He taught that his father's house should be a prayer house for the nations but it has been made a place of thieves. This was not popular behaviour at a major religious festival. The religious leaders questioned his authority, tried to trap him and continued to plot his death.

On the way into the temple one day, one of the disciples notices the huge stones and comments on the magnificence of the building (Mark 13). Mark tactfully does not record which disciple it was! Magnificent as the buildings were they were nothing compared with the events that were about to unfold. The day of the temple in Jerusalem being the focus of worship of God's people is about to pass. The time is coming when people will worship in spirit and in truth, when there will be a new high priest and when the church universal as the body of Christ will become the glory of God. Jesus is explicit in his prophecy that the temple will be physically demolished, an event which takes place in AD70. He goes on to describe other events of deception, tribulation, persecution and suffering that will take place at that time and in the future. Some of the things spoken about in Mark 13 refer to the immediate future, others to the events preceding Jesus' return.

Two key points are emphasized: if people stand firm they will be saved and they should not be deceived by anyone claiming to be the Christ. Following Jesus is not a crutch or a soft option. At the start of the 21st Century there are Christians being imprisoned, persecuted, tortured and killed because of their faith in Jesus. Jesus tells the disciples that they should expect this to get worse – but that it won't last forever.

The second coming
History is going to come to an end. Time is linear and the story has a conclusion.

Jesus is going to return in power and glory, not quietly, like the first time, but suddenly and publicly. This is definitely going to happen. No one knows precisely when Jesus is coming back. We live now in what the Bible calls the last days – the time period between Jesus' first and second coming. The way to live well in these days is not in idle speculation but in preparation.

One of the things the terrorist attack in September 2001 did was to remind me of the impermanence of life. It looked like those twin towers would last forever and yet in just a few hours they were gone. I have spent some time in New York since then and have spoken to a number of people who are quite clear that they would have lived differently that day had they known what was going to happen. Jesus is coming back. There is a going to be a new heaven and a new earth. Jesus' kingdom is the present and the future.

There are two short parables towards the end of Mark 13: the lesson of the fig tree is to 'watch the signs' and that of the householder is to 'be prepared'. If we know what is going to happen in the future it should change our perspective on life now. Tragically, many leave it too late and continue as if they are invincible and indestructible. I have a long standing fascination with the Titanic. It was the finest engineering feat of its generation, deemed unsinkable. Just before midnight on April 14th 1912 it struck an ice berg. Many passengers refused to believe that anything serious was happening and continued with their conversations, games or entertainment. The Titanic took almost two and a half hours to sink, by the time the urgency of the situation had been grasped it was too late. The inadequate provision of lifeboats is well documented. 1500 people lost their lives but more could have been saved. Only lifeboat number 11 was filled to capacity. Sadly, today many continue in the staterooms of their lives, believing there to be little danger and plenty of time. Please do not allow yourself to be lulled into a false sense of security. There are two things we know for sure about the future. First, Jesus will return and, second, we will all face God's judgement. How do you feel about that?

What a waste?

While Jesus was staying in Bethany near Jerusalem a woman came while he was reclining at the table (Mark 14). She took a very expensive bottle of pure nard. Normally this would be used to anoint the corpse of a dead person. She broke the bottle, poured some over his head and anointed his body. This did not go down well with some of the others who objected to what they saw as a colossal waste of money. They even argued that the money should have gone to the poor. Jesus rebuked them and affirmed that what she was doing was right. This woman spent a year's salary in a few minutes. Her love for Jesus was extravagant; she realized who he was and wanted to express her appreciation. There was also a prophetic aspect to this act – the perfume used was usually reserved for the anointing of dead bodies. The woman seemed to sense what he was going to do. Jesus is deeply touched by her affection.

Who are you with on this one? On the one hand the disciples seem to have a point – why waste something valuable on Jesus when it could have been used for a variety of more useful purposes. On the other hand, here is a woman who takes the best of what she has and pours it out for Jesus' sake. In the final analysis genuine love cannot be reduced to economic formula. Emperor Shah Jehan who built the Taj

Mahal could have spent the money on improving roads. Instead of buying my wife flowers I could put the money towards children's clothes. You can certainly debate the issues, but what is not in doubt is that Jehan and I love truly and deeply. The Taj stands as a great memorial to his love, the flowers on the table a more transient testimony to mine (although my kids do have something to wear!). The woman's offering is a memorial to her great love of Jesus. Do you love Jesus like that? Come to think of it – do I?

Passover

Being Scottish there are three events which broadly speaking define my cultural identity. 1314 Bannockburn (they'll never take our freedom!), 1745 Culloden (they take our freedom), 1978 Argentina (they are not crying with us they are crying at us). There are of course many more positive events which have shaped my nation (it's just hard to think of them!)

One of the defining moments in the history of Israel was the Exodus. The people of Israel were rescued from slavery and oppression in Egypt and embarked on an epic journey to the Promised Land. The night before the Exodus, God sent a plague on the first born sons of the families of Egypt. It was a dreadful and decisive night when Pharaoh finally said that the Israelites could leave Egypt. Moses told the people that when the plague came they would be safe if they followed God's instructions. Lamb's blood was to be daubed on the lintel of each house so that when death came it would see the blood and 'pass over' the houses with blood on the doors. The enactment of this last meal as the people prepared to leave and the thankfulness for God's delivery from death became the focus of the Passover feast, which is still as significant in Judaism today as it was in Jesus' day.

Jesus takes the disciples to an upper room to celebrate the feast together. The room may have belonged to Mark's family. Everything goes as expected until Jesus suddenly starts talking about his betrayal. Then, instead of talking about the lamb, he begins talking about himself, about his body being broken and his blood poured out. Jesus uses the Passover meal to throw light on what is about to happen. Blood will save from death once more – not the blood of a lamb, but his very own. God's new covenant, promised long ago, will be signed and sealed in blood. The significance of this will only be seen fully later but for now notice that Christ's body will be broken and his blood 'poured out for many'. There is purpose and intention here – it is premeditated. Jesus knows what he has to do and why. This is what he has come to do, this is what he was born for, this is the fulfilment of his mission – to die.

Up for the cup

Jesus takes Peter, James and John to the garden at Gethsemane (Mark 14.32–42). He knows that the final hour of his betrayal is almost upon him. He prays in the garden to his father. The form and substance of his prayer give us a unique insight into the nature of God and what is about to happen on the cross.

Jesus calls God his father but he addresses him in a uniquely personal way. The term '*Abba*' is essentially an informal family term. It is a bit like 'Daddy' or 'Papa' in my culture. The use of this language underlines again the intimacy in the Godhead. The Father loves the Son, his only beloved son, the Son loves the Father and is willing that the Father's will be done in his life. It is this closeness of community which is going to be the pain of the cross. God is a great God of love. Jesus prays about the cup he is going to have to drink. This completes the other part of the equation. The cup in Old Testament times was an image used to symbolize God's wrath. God's righteous anger against sin is proclaimed thus in the book of Isaiah:

> *Awake, awake!*
>   *Rise up, O Jerusalem,*
> *you who have drunk from the hand of the Lord*
>   *the cup of his wrath,*
> *you who have drained to its dregs the goblet that*
>   *makes men stagger* (Isaiah 51.17)

Or again in the book of Jeremiah:

> *This is what the Lord, the God of Israel, said to me: 'Take from my hand this cup filled with the wine of my wrath and make all the nations to whom I send you drink it.'* (Jeremiah 25.15)

God is righteous and holy, loving and just. Sin can have no place. God is far from ambivalent towards sin. His wrath and anger preserve the integrity of his character.

The penalty for sin is death. Human beings are all living under a death sentence. A verdict has already been passed and it is a capital one. Everywhere you turn in universities and colleges, in offices and shops, in hospitals, or schools or public services you can see 'dead men and women walking'.

We are all living on death row. It is not in doubt that you are going to die. The only question is how much time do you have left? Now I know this is not a comfortable thought but stay with me for a minute. Imagine you are on death row and somebody comes and tells you that they are willing to take your place. It is a preposterous idea – what kind of idiot would die in your place? Who could be willing to do such a thing? Rumours fly about the prison. Some have heard it is a famous rock star, others a top sportsman, a wealthy business man, a head of state or a great religious leader. It seems incredible and then you recognize who it is. It's Pele, Paul McCartney, Bill Gates, President Bush – only it's not any of them. It is someone much more important.

Walking to the death, to which you have been sentenced, is the only son of the Living God, the perfect and pure Jesus Christ. It is utterly shocking that God in his enormous love and mercy was willing to do this. The righteous Jesus faced the penalty that unrighteous you deserved. Your unright-eousness has now been paid for, the punishment has been served. If you are willing to accept this transaction then you are free. But more than that – his righteousness can be cred-ited to you so that you are not just free but are put right with God. Did you notice the cautionary note there? I said, 'If you are willing'. You have the option of declining the offer of substitution and taking that last walk yourself. Maybe some-thing will happen, a last minute reprieve or perhaps you can earn a pardon by good behaviour – and in any case you can't accept that Jesus did this for you. But there can be no reprieve – God is just and cannot turn a blind eye. You cannot work your way out of it. If you could, you wouldn't be on death row in the first place. Jesus is your only hope.

Besides we are talking about more than avoiding death here. We are talking about the free gift of eternal life and that is in God's hands. We are talking about you being declared right with God which is by his power and word. We are also talking about the indwelling and help of the Holy Spirit which is God's initiative.

Jesus took on himself the full punishment for the sins of the world

> ⁹*This is how God showed his love among us: He sent his one and only Son into the world that we might live through him.* ¹⁰*This is love: not that we loved God, but that he loved us and sent his Son as an atoning sacrifice for our sins.* (1 John 4.9,10)

So wrote John, the disciple of Jesus, decades later. Another John, John the Baptist, introduced Jesus as 'The lamb of God who takes away the sin of the world.' Jesus does this by offering himself in our stead. Would you rather face God's righteous judgement, knowing that your accounts had been settled by Jesus, or would you prefer to give it a whirl on your own? Jesus faced God's punishment and died so that you didn't have to. Has anyone loved you like this before?

Amnesty
When Jesus was arrested there was someone on death row, a convicted terrorist named Barabbus who had taken part in a

recent uprising where he had committed murder. Pilate is unable to find grounds for conviction against Jesus. Pilate is an astute enough politician to recognize what is going on and thinks that he may be able to use the crowd to trump the jealousy of the chief priests. After all it is less than a week since the triumphal entry of Jesus into the city, which had been front page news. It was the custom at that festival weekend for Pilate to release one prisoner to the crowd by popular demand. He suggests releasing Jesus but the chief priests stir up the crowd into a mob who demand the release of Barabbus and the crucifixion of Jesus. The guilty Barabbus walks free, while the innocent Jesus is taken away to be flogged and crucified. The most significant events in human history are about to unfold.

The cross and resurrection

Crucifixion was a particularly painful and protracted form of public execution. Mark does not go into the details – it was not something to be dwelled upon. Frequently victims carried their own crossbeam to the place of execution. On arrival they were stripped naked and their arms were tied or nailed through the wrist to the cross beam. This was fixed to the top of a vertical stake. Death was caused by asphyxiation when the victim no longer had enough strength to keep pushing up their body weight to be able to breathe. Sometimes the victims' legs were broken late in the day to precipitate the end. It was a horrible and humiliating way to die and Roman citizens could not be crucified.

It was common practice for the crime of the victim to be written above them. Jesus dies with a sign above his head saying the King of the Jews (Mark 15.26). The Jewish authorities object but Pilate sticks to his guns. He intends a certain irony but there are other ironies: the one who will judge all things stands before a court which cannot even judge itself; the God of glory is given a robe and crown and mocked by the soldiers who even perform a sort of coronation. Jesus' willingness to endure these extreme caricatures of reality is a further testimony to the reality of who he is.

The cross on the hill not the sermon on the mount is the enduring symbol of the Christian faith. This is where access to God is opened up by the death of Jesus. Even the weather seems sympathetic to the events taking place – the darkness is symbolic of separation and sin. The sixth hour is noon, so from midday until 3pm, when the sun should have been at its hottest and brightest, darkness shrouded the land.

Jesus in his death knew the anguish of a condemned man. The agonies inflicted were not just by the hands of Romans but by the hand of his father as the wrath of God is poured out.

On top of the Old Bailey in London is the golden statue of *Justicia* holding the scales of justice in one hand and a sword in the other. The message is clear: those found guilty in the scales of justice will experience the punishment of the sword. God's wrath is the consequence of his justice. We have been weighed and found guilty and the deserved punishment is carried out. Amazingly not on us but on Jesus. Peter later describes it like this 'Christ also suffered once for sins, the righteous for the unrighteous, to bring you to God.' 1 Peter 3.18. We are put right with God by faith in Jesus and what he has done on the cross.

Access all areas

In the temple in Jerusalem there were two curtains. These were huge hangings more like stud partition walls than drapes 10 metres high and 15 centimetres thick. The first separated the court of the Gentiles from the sanctuary, in other words the place where the public could go from the place where only the people of God were allowed. The second separated off the 'Holy of Holies', the place where in Judaism the presence of God was deemed to be in a particular way. The high priest could only enter this place once a year on the Day of Atonement. Such was the fear of the holiness and glory of God that when the priest went in he had bells on his garments and a rope tied round his waist. If the bells were not ringing the rope was there to haul out his dead body.

We are not sure which curtain was torn when Jesus died – both have an obvious symbolism in proclaiming that the way to God is now open. Some argue that the outer curtain was the more visible and public sign but with the huge impact of the inner curtain ripping it could hardly be a kept a secret. My understanding is that it is more likely to be the inner curtain but you can pay your money and take your choice. The curtain was ripped from top to bottom. It is God who opens the way and who opens it wide. It also symbolizes that access to God is now open in a new way – because Jesus died in our place the way to God is now clear.

These religious leaders were not convinced. They mocked Jesus on the cross and had the curtain repaired. They were the ones who knew the way to God and Jesus was not part of the equation. The barrier between God and humanity was reinstated. They had a system for gaining access to God and it didn't involve the cross.

The first response of conviction comes from an unlikely source. As far as we can gather it was like any other crucifixion for the soldiers involved. They flogged the victim, nailed him to the cross and gambled over his possessions. They were busy with their daily lives and failed to appreciate the significance of what was going on above their heads.

One man notices that something extraordinary is taking place. The tough Roman centurion sees Jesus die and without a hint of irony, acknowledges that this was indeed the son of God. As Jesus dies we are reminded of the first words Mark wrote about Jesus being the son of God.

This death was not a tragedy but the deliberate fulfilment of God's rescue plan. Here we witness the character of Jesus.

These events on the cross are for me and for you. We rebel against the God who created us; each of us has turned to our own way. But that rebellion is not the end. God did not abandon us and God has not abandoned us. He came after us. Jesus Christ did not come to condemn us but to save us. God has drawn alongside us in Jesus, entering into our situation and identifying with us. Jesus knows what it's like to be lonely, scared, misunderstood and rejected. Identifying with us in his life was the precursor to identifying with us in his death. He died that we might live.

My friend will pay

The first four words you should learn in any foreign language when you are travelling are the only four words which will do you any good on the day of judgement. Once or twice I have asked people what they think these words should be. They suggest things like 'I am very sorry' – but this is hopeless when you are travelling and too late on the day of judgement. Another is, 'I tried my best', which is just as useless for travelling and inadequate on the day of day of judgement. The first four words you should learn in any language – which are the only four words which will do you any good on judgement day – are 'My friend will pay'.

Tremendously useful when travelling with an unsuspecting companion.

An ideal phrase to have ready in a restaurant or bar!

But also the only words with which we can face judgement.

Our friend Jesus has paid. My friend Jesus will pay.

Jesus has done it. Jesus has lived the righteous life required by God that we are unable to do. There is a great hymn which starts, 'The price is paid! Come let us enter in to all that Jesus died to make his own!' Who is going to settle your account with God? Is it your intention to try yourself or to ask Jesus?

In the movie *Saving Private Ryan*, Captain John Miller leads a squad to rescue the eponymous hero. Miller dies but accomplishes his mission and Ryan is saved (this may be yet another movie I have ruined for you). With his dying breath Miller, conscious of the great cost and sacrifice that have gone into saving Ryan whispers 'Earn this'. The final scene of the film takes place in the present with Ryan at Miller's grave. 'Everyday I think about what you said to me on that bridge. I've tried to live my life the best I could. I hope that was enough. I hope that at least in your eyes I've earned what all of you have done for me.' He turns to his wife with tears in his eyes and pleads, 'Tell me I have led a good life, tell me I'm a good man'. It is a moving and poignant climax to the movie but reveals a terrible burden carried for fifty years.

These ideas of earning salvation and trying your best are not unique to war films. The religions of the world are based on these very ideas. Religion is about humanity in search of God, trying to earn approval or reward by our own efforts. Jesus is God in search of human beings, doing what we could never do, to bring us to himself. The message of Jesus is not 'earn this', it is 'receive this'. We can never earn what God has done for us in sending Jesus to die in our place.

This is not a 'get out of jail free' card. It is a pardon. There is now no condemnation for those who are in Christ. Are you ready to receive this pardon or are you going to keep trying to earn it.

Resurrection

The story is told of a Cambridge College where on registration you had to state your religious affiliation. If you put 'Christian', as the majority did for mostly cultural rather than spiritual reasons, you were expected to be at compulsory chapel at 8am. One new student, not fancying the prospect, entered 'sun worshipper' as his religion. Congratulating himself on his cleverness and looking forward to a lie-in he was shocked to discover the Master of the College knocking on his door at 5am. 'The sun will be rising in ten minutes and I expect you to be up to welcome it into a new day.' At that moment the student started to think, 'I have to get a new religion'. His choice was based on ease, not on convictions about the truth. Truth is never true just because you want it to be.

There are many different ideas about what happened after

the crucifixion. I firmly believe that the resurrection is the only sustainable explanation for what happened.

There are three big issues in the resurrection:

The empty tomb. How did a closely guarded tomb with a huge stone rolled across its entrance come to be empty? It is inconceivable that Jesus was not really dead and somehow after his ordeal could have pulled this off himself. Equally implausible is the notion that the disciples went to the wrong tomb. Even when you are upset you don't make mistakes like that.

The missing body. If the Jews or the Romans took it for some reason why was it never produced? The disciples are claiming that Jesus was alive – producing the body would be a fairly effective rebuttal tactic. Moreover there is to this day no known resting place of Jesus. If the disciples had somehow managed to snatch the corpse they would surely have venerated the grave of their leader.

The witnesses. Jesus was seen alive on eleven occasions after his resurrection in the gospel accounts. This was not a hallucination. Paul writing to the Corinthian church pointed out that over 500 people saw Jesus, many of whom were still alive at the time of writing.

Not one of these is conclusive on its own but together they produce persuasive evidence. It is not the most comfortable conclusion but it may be the truth.

We are clearly told that it was a physical resurrection, and that the first to discover what was going on were afraid. For me, one of the most compelling proofs has been what happened to turn those frightened lives around. At no personal gain, they started spreading this story that Jesus was alive. They faced persecution and death and not one of them

ever changed their story. It is not so hard to die for a lie –
many do so having been sincerely deluded. But to die for a lie
of your own invention is almost unheard of.

What do you think happened after the crucifixion? Could
Jesus be alive?

And finally…

I wonder what you think at this point. Perhaps you still
believe that this is all very interesting but it's basically an
invention, a projection, even a deception, a feel-good
mythology, misguided dependency or misplaced wish-fulfil-
ment. Maybe you don't think it matters if it is – it's harmless if
it helps me – but it's not for you. It is the resurrection that
supremely stands as an indictment of that kind of thinking. If
Jesus did not rise from the dead then I am investing my life in
a lie, I am being consoled by a false hope and an empty illu-
sion. If Jesus did not rise from the dead you should not be
humouring me, you should be helping me.

The Apostle Paul understood this completely: 'if Christ has
not been raised … we are to be pitied more than all others' (1
Corinthians 15.17,19). The Christian faith only has validity if
it has reality and only reality if it has veracity. Either the world
was created or it wasn't, either God exists or he doesn't,
humanity is fashioned in his image or we aren't, Jesus is who
he said he was or he wasn't, the resurrection happened or it
didn't.

It is not always easy to resolve these issues and there are
clearly many other ideas and opinions in all of these areas.
The resurrection means you have to give Jesus a good look. If
it happened it means three things: his death on the cross for

sin was accepted by God and his is the only name by which we can be saved; he is alive today and can be known personally (you can know 'about' other figures but you can know Jesus); and he is coming back one day in power and majesty. If the resurrection is a myth or invention, frankly I do not think I have anything to say worth listening to about Jesus.

My favourite text book at University finished abruptly. The last page said something to the effect of, 'I have finished this book in a hurry, the situation is desperate, I cannot write while my people suffer. I am off to the barricades'. I found this refreshing and sometimes wondered why more professors hadn't finished their books in a hurry and gone to the barricades. At times it would have made my situation less desperate. Mark is writing in desperate times and finishes his gospel in a hurry.

It is not even clear what his original ending was from a number of alternative early fragments. Much is left to the other gospel writers to describe in greater detail. The abrupt way Mark finishes also serves to turn the focus on the reader. How are you going to respond to this? How is this story going to be continued? It is not a comfortable ending with all the loose ends tidied away. It is a messy ending which calls us to a response.

God's unconditional love brings us to a point of change

The reality of Jesus presents the most significant decision that any of us have to make in our lives. It is not possible to be ambivalent about this man. Either we must decide to love and follow him with our whole hearts or we decide to turn our back on him and continue to live life for ourselves. There is absolutely no room for neutrality – we are either for Jesus or against him. The choice is yours.

I hope as you have read Mark's gospel you have begun to appreciate that Jesus is for you. God in his great mercy and unfathomable love has demonstrated the full extent of his commitment.

Because of who he is – the Son of God, his only son – and what he has done – died and rose again.

Jesus still comes to us today with this question: Who do you say that I am?

God loves you unconditionally. That does not mean that there is nothing that you need to do to respond to God. God's love is not about making you feel better about yourself. Jesus did not die to make you feel better but to reconcile you to God. He has done everything that is necessary to bring you into a new relationship with the living God that will last for eternity. God longs to adopt us as his children, to be our heavenly father and to give us an inheritance for eternity. If we are going to live like this it will only be possible through the help of the Holy Spirit. He does, however, call us to a life where there is nothing we keep enclosed away from God.

John Newton was a former slave trader who hit rock bottom and met Jesus. The hymn he wrote describing his experiences has become a classic.

> Amazing Grace how sweet the sound
> That saved a wretch like me
> I once was lost but now am found
> Was blind but now I see

He appreciated that he had been saved by grace alone. God's undeserved and rich mercy had come to him. No one is beyond the reach of God's grace. Someone described grace as understanding 'I am more wicked than I ever realized, but I'm also more loved than I ever dreamed.' God loves you and even though you do not deserve it he offers you forgiveness, reconciliation, life and hope.

With all my heart I implore you. Be reconciled to God!

Meet Jesus

One of my favourite times of the academic year is freshers' week. It is exciting seeing students embark on a new phase of life together and amusing to witness the conversations. During freshers' weeks you hear the same questions repeated time and time again.

'What is your name?'

'Where are you from?'

'What are you doing here?'

'Would you like a free gift?'

It is a time when students are understandably keen to meet as many new people as possible and when they are offered a fair amount of free stuff.

When I started University I could have had a tee shirt printed saying 'Nigel. Edinburgh. English. Yes please'. Had my fellow students done the same it would almost have eliminated the need for conversation at all.

I got to wondering what would happen if a student met Jesus in that kind of framework. How would the conversation go?

What would you say to Jesus?

What is your name?

Jesus Christ.

Where are you from?

Well originally I was in heaven. Through me and for me all things were made. My life was the light of humanity. Then I came to earth, I was born of a virgin, lived thirty years as a carpenter man and boy. After three years of public ministry I was crucified on a cross for the sins of the world. Three days later God brought me back to life again. Then I ascended into heaven, where I am now seated at the right hand of God from where I will come in the future to judge the living and the dead and usher in a glorious new kingdom which will last forever.

Wow – I'm from Edinburgh!

What are you doing here?

I am doing what I always do. Seeking and saving the lost. Reconciling men and women to the God who made them and knows them and loves them and longs for them to come home.

Would you like a free gift?

What have you got?

Not much really.

What would Jesus say to you?

I know your name.

I know where you are from, I know everything about you.

I know what you are doing here. I brought you to this place.

Your life is not random.

Would you like a free gift?

The free gift of God is eternal life in Christ Jesus.

You encountering Jesus is not hypothetical – it is a real possibility. We have his written promise in the Bible – that if we seek him with all our hearts we will find him.

Perhaps there is still more for you to check out. You know you are getting closer to turning to Jesus but are not quite there yet. Can I encourage you to keep searching? Read more of the Bible for yourself, perhaps another gospel or Paul's letter to the Romans.

You may have a friend who can recommend a good church or take you to 'Christianity Explored' or an 'Alpha' course. There may be some special event where you can find out more. Please take this opportunity to thoroughly investigate the Christian faith.

Perhaps if you have come this far you are ready to go a little bit further. You know that God has been speaking to you. You may be ready to become a Christian. Even if you are not yet at that point, it may be interesting to know how that happens.

It is really very simple. You talk to God. Praying is not about long words and religious language. You just talk to God in your own words. It may feel a little strange at first but God will hear you. I find it helpful to use an 'ABCD' pattern.

A

Admit that you are under God's righteous judgement, that you have turned your back on him, that you have not loved him with all your heart, soul and strength. Acknowledge that you have fallen short of God's perfect standard and that you are unable to face his righteous judgement. You need rescue.

B

Believe that Jesus died for you. 'God demonstrates his own

love for us in this: While we were still sinners Christ died for us.' (Romans 5.8) Jesus on the cross bore the sins of the world. His death was the penalty we deserve and you want to be counted in to that. You want to face God's judgement not on your life but on his. Jesus is the rescuer.

C

Count the cost. Are you willing to accept Jesus as your saviour and authority over you? God never forces himself upon you. Loving him will not be easy. Putting God first in your life will be a major challenge for whomever or whatever is in that position at the moment. Following Jesus is not a crutch – it may involve misunderstanding and persecution. It will involve a new direction and a new set of priorities. 'Whoever would be my disciple must deny self, take up their cross and follow me.' (see Mark 8.34–37). Are you ready for this?

D

Decide. God brings us to a point of decision. You need to decide to accept or reject Jesus. There is no middle ground; a decision to delay making a decision is to reject him. You may in God's grace and mercy get another opportunity but life is uncertain and there are no guarantees. What is stopping you from becoming a Christian? If you are ready to respond to God, talk to him. You do not need to use special language; God knows you and will hear you.

Thank him, confess your sin to him, and invite him to become your Saviour, Lord and God.

You may find it helpful to use the following short prayer as a starting point.

Dear God

Thank you for speaking to me from your word.

I admit that I have been living my life without you. I have fallen short of your perfect standard in thought, word and deed. I realize that I cannot please you by my own efforts.

I believe that Jesus died on the cross for me. Thank you for your great love and mercy.

I surrender control of my life to you. Please forgive my sins. I ask you now to come into my life to be my saviour, Lord and God from this day forward.

Please send the Holy Spirit to cleanse me and help me. I receive Him now.

Please help me to live as your child, as part of your family. I know I still have a lot to learn but thank you that right now I know eternity is secure. Enable me to live for you and with you each day.

Amen

You may find it helpful to reflect on a verse from the Bible:

> [8]*For it is by grace you have been saved, through faith – and this is not from yourselves, it is the gift of God –* [9]*not by works, so that no-one can boast.* [10]*For we are God's handi-work, created in Christ Jesus to do good works, which God prepared in advance for us to do.* (Ephesians 2.8–10)

Becoming a Christian is a simple transaction that has profound consequences. On 11 August 1990 two young people stood at the front of a church. Promises were made, rings were given and received, our friends and families celebrated. Our relationship changed immediately, we were no longer engaged – we were married, our relationship had a different legal status, we had entered into a new level of commitment. All this had happened as a result of this brief transaction that took place between us. We didn't know everything about each other – we still don't! We didn't know all that lay ahead. Saying 'yes' to Ailsa was the end of one phase of life and the beginning of something new and exciting. In all honesty I did not really know what I was letting myself in for but it has turned out to be the second best decision I have made in my life. The best was the decision some years before to accept Jesus as my Saviour, Lord and God.

Are you ready to make that decision?

What is on offer is a new relationship with God through faith in Jesus Christ.

What is at stake is your eternal destiny and the fruitfulness of your life now and in the future.

Will you say yes to Jesus?